Introduction

Welcome to this workbook and thank you for supporting buying this. ☺

I'm constantly telling you the best way to learn is by practising questions, so I've made you a book full of practice questions.

Your GCSE maths is divided in to five different topics, there will be a different number of questions (or parts of questions) depending on the topic. The different number of questions in each section in the first section of this book reflects the exam.

15% Number	8 questions
20% Ratio, Proportion and Rate of Change	10 questions
30% Algebra	15 questions
15% Statistics and Probability	7 questions
20% Geometry and Measure	10 questions

The second 50 questions are all algebra based, algebra makes up the basis for a large number of questions so it is essential that you know it all confidently.

This book is **not** designed as a text book or revision guide, but as a workbook. There are lots of good (and bad) expensive and free revision guides out there, on my YouTube channel and other great websites. So, there is no point in me adding to the masses.

All the teaching, all the new content, is available for free on my YouTube channel, this book is for you to practice and learn. The best way to approach this is to watch the teaching video and make notes, or after class try a section and check the answers.

Any corrections that are needed after the book is published will be listed on my website, www.primrosekitten.com these will be corrected in the next version of the book

Other books in this series

Previously published...
- Maths and Calculator skills for Science Students — March 2016
- Maths (The Chemistry bits) for GCSE Combined Science — May 2016
- Maths (The Chemistry bits) for GCSE Triple Science — May 2016
  http://amzn.to/2vgQCRf
- Science revision Guide — April 2017
- Maths Revision Guide — April 2017
- Summer Start for A-Level Chemistry — May 2017
  http://amzn.to/2suR1e5
- Atoms, Electrons, Structure and Bonding Workbook — June 2017
  http://amzn.to/2tn8Rji
- 75 long answers questions in GCSE science — April 2018
  https://amzn.to/2HvvxUU

Coming soon...
- Organic Chemistry Workbook
- Maths for A-Level Chemistry
- Maths (The Physics bits) for GCSE Combined Science
- Maths (The Physics bits) for GCSE Triple Science
- Summer Start for A-Level Physics

Chances are if you want a maths/science book I've written it or I am writing it.

For full book listings visit www.PrimroseKitten.com and follow @primrose_kitten

First published 2017   Copyright; Primrose Kitten ©

Image credits, Images, used under license from Shutterstock.com.

Acknowledgements
Thank you to my husband for putting up with my spending every night writing this and for correcting all of my SPG mistakes. To my sons for being the inspiration behind Primrose Kitten.

Contents

Introduction 1
Other books in this series 2
Contents 3
Number Learning Objectives 5
Algebra Learning Objectives 7
Ratio, Proportion and Rates of Change Learning Objectives 10
Geometry and Measures Learning Objectives 12
Probability Learning Objectives 16
Statistics Learning Objectives 17
15% Number 18
20% Ratio, Proportion and Rate of Change 21
30% Algebra 26
15% Statistics and Probability 32
20% Geometry and Measure 35
Algebra Book 2 41
Answers 49

For a summary of the Whole of GCSE Maths in 2 hours https://youtu.be/dYPwEyeyPLA

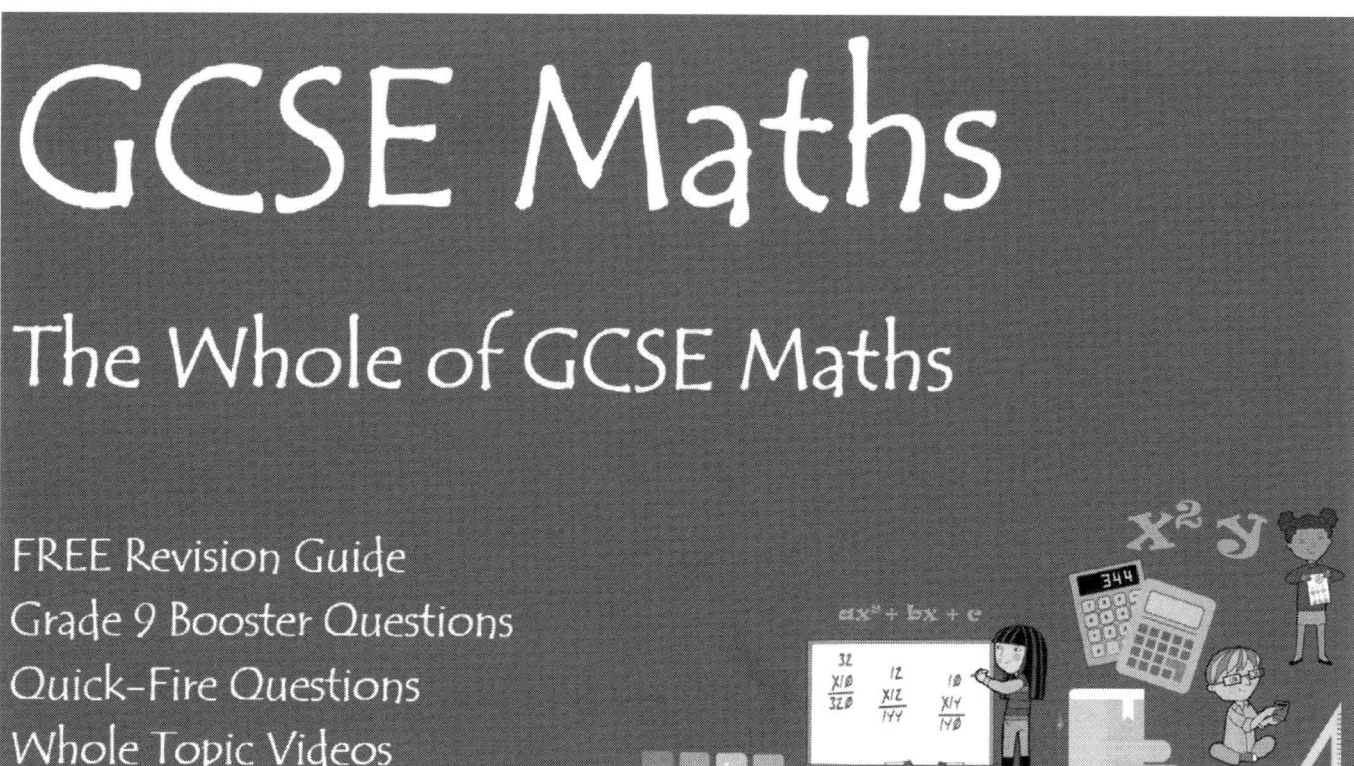

Number Learning Objectives

Specification statement These are the bits the exam board wants you to know, make sure you can do all of these...	Self-assessment		
	First review 4-7 months before exam	Second review 1-2 months before exam	Final review Week before exam
I can define the term integer	☺ 😐 ☹	☺ 😐 ☹	☺ 😐 ☹
I can order positive integers	☺ 😐 ☹	☺ 😐 ☹	☺ 😐 ☹
I can order negative integers	☺ 😐 ☹	☺ 😐 ☹	☺ 😐 ☹
I can order fractions	☺ 😐 ☹	☺ 😐 ☹	☺ 😐 ☹
I can order decimals	☺ 😐 ☹	☺ 😐 ☹	☺ 😐 ☹
I can use =, ≠, <, >, ≤, ≥	☺ 😐 ☹	☺ 😐 ☹	☺ 😐 ☹
I can define the mathematical term operation	☺ 😐 ☹	☺ 😐 ☹	☺ 😐 ☹
I can add, subtract, divide and multiply integers	☺ 😐 ☹	☺ 😐 ☹	☺ 😐 ☹
I can add, subtract, divide and multiply fractions	☺ 😐 ☹	☺ 😐 ☹	☺ 😐 ☹
I can add, subtract, divide and multiply decimals	☺ 😐 ☹	☺ 😐 ☹	☺ 😐 ☹
I can order operations; and identify which should be used first.	☺ 😐 ☹	☺ 😐 ☹	☺ 😐 ☹
I can recognise opposite operations	☺ 😐 ☹	☺ 😐 ☹	☺ 😐 ☹
I can define and identify prime numbers	☺ 😐 ☹	☺ 😐 ☹	☺ 😐 ☹
I can define and identify factors	☺ 😐 ☹	☺ 😐 ☹	☺ 😐 ☹
I can define and identify multiples	☺ 😐 ☹	☺ 😐 ☹	☺ 😐 ☹
I can define and identify common factors	☺ 😐 ☹	☺ 😐 ☹	☺ 😐 ☹
I can define and identify common multiples	☺ 😐 ☹	☺ 😐 ☹	☺ 😐 ☹
I can define and identify highest common factor (HCF)	☺ 😐 ☹	☺ 😐 ☹	☺ 😐 ☹
I can define and identify lowest common multiple (LCM)	☺ 😐 ☹	☺ 😐 ☹	☺ 😐 ☹
I can define and identify prime factorisation	☺ 😐 ☹	☺ 😐 ☹	☺ 😐 ☹
I can identify and calculate square numbers	☺ 😐 ☹	☺ 😐 ☹	☺ 😐 ☹
I can identify and calculate cube numbers	☺ 😐 ☹	☺ 😐 ☹	☺ 😐 ☹
I can identify and calculate square roots	☺ 😐 ☹	☺ 😐 ☹	☺ 😐 ☹
I can identify and calculate cube roots	☺ 😐 ☹	☺ 😐 ☹	☺ 😐 ☹
I can calculate powers of 4 or higher	☺ 😐 ☹	☺ 😐 ☹	☺ 😐 ☹
I can calculate roots	☺ 😐 ☹	☺ 😐 ☹	☺ 😐 ☹
I can calculate using fractions	☺ 😐 ☹	☺ 😐 ☹	☺ 😐 ☹
I can calculate using π	☺ 😐 ☹	☺ 😐 ☹	☺ 😐 ☹

Primrose Kitten - YouTube Tutorials for Science and Maths.

I can calculate and interpret standard form	☺ 😐 ☹	☺ 😐 ☹	☺ 😐 ☹
I can convert fractions to decimals and decimals to fractions **Flashcards to help with this available to download from www.primrosekitten.com**	☺ 😐 ☹	☺ 😐 ☹	☺ 😐 ☹
I can use fractions in ratios	☺ 😐 ☹	☺ 😐 ☹	☺ 😐 ☹
I can use percentages	☺ 😐 ☹	☺ 😐 ☹	☺ 😐 ☹
I can recall and convert standard units for mass	☺ 😐 ☹	☺ 😐 ☹	☺ 😐 ☹
I can recall and convert standard units for time	☺ 😐 ☹	☺ 😐 ☹	☺ 😐 ☹
I can recall and convert standard units for length	☺ 😐 ☹	☺ 😐 ☹	☺ 😐 ☹
I can recall and convert standard units for money	☺ 😐 ☹	☺ 😐 ☹	☺ 😐 ☹
I can use estimation to calculate quantities	☺ 😐 ☹	☺ 😐 ☹	☺ 😐 ☹
I can round numbers to a specified number of decimal places or significant figures	☺ 😐 ☹	☺ 😐 ☹	☺ 😐 ☹
I can use inequalities to show the interval a number might fall between	☺ 😐 ☹	☺ 😐 ☹	☺ 😐 ☹
I can interpret limits of accuracy	☺ 😐 ☹	☺ 😐 ☹	☺ 😐 ☹
Higher tier only			
I can estimate powers and roots for a given positive number	☺ 😐 ☹	☺ 😐 ☹	☺ 😐 ☹
I can calculate with surds	☺ 😐 ☹	☺ 😐 ☹	☺ 😐 ☹
I can simplify expression involving surds	☺ 😐 ☹	☺ 😐 ☹	☺ 😐 ☹
I can change recurring decimals to fractions and fractions in to recurring decimals	☺ 😐 ☹	☺ 😐 ☹	☺ 😐 ☹
I can determine upper and lower bound of accuracy	☺ 😐 ☹	☺ 😐 ☹	☺ 😐 ☹
I can use the product rule for counting	☺ 😐 ☹	☺ 😐 ☹	☺ 😐 ☹
I can estimate powers and roots for a given positive number	☺ 😐 ☹	☺ 😐 ☹	☺ 😐 ☹
I can use fractional indices	☺ 😐 ☹	☺ 😐 ☹	☺ 😐 ☹

Algebra Learning Objectives

Specification statement These are the bits the exam board wants you to know, make sure you can do all of these...	Self-assessment		
	First review 4-7 months before exam	Second review 1-2 months before exam	Final review Week before exam
I can recognise that $a \times b$ is equal to ab	☺ 😐 ☹	☺ 😐 ☹	☺ 😐 ☹
I can recognise that $4a$ is equal to $a + a + a + a$ or $4 \times a$	☺ 😐 ☹	☺ 😐 ☹	☺ 😐 ☹
I can recognise that y^2 is equal to $y \times y$	☺ 😐 ☹	☺ 😐 ☹	☺ 😐 ☹
I can recognise that $\frac{a}{b}$ is equal to $a \div b$	☺ 😐 ☹	☺ 😐 ☹	☺ 😐 ☹
I can use $a \times b$ is equal to ab	☺ 😐 ☹	☺ 😐 ☹	☺ 😐 ☹
I can use $4a$ is equal to $a + a + a + a$ or $4 \times a$	☺ 😐 ☹	☺ 😐 ☹	☺ 😐 ☹
I can use y^2 is equal to $y \times y$	☺ 😐 ☹	☺ 😐 ☹	☺ 😐 ☹
I can use $\frac{a}{b}$ is equal to $a \div b$	☺ 😐 ☹	☺ 😐 ☹	☺ 😐 ☹
I can put numbers into an algebraic expression and if needed calculate an answer	☺ 😐 ☹	☺ 😐 ☹	☺ 😐 ☹
I can collect like terms in an algebraic expression	☺ 😐 ☹	☺ 😐 ☹	☺ 😐 ☹
I can multiply out a number in front of a bracket	☺ 😐 ☹	☺ 😐 ☹	☺ 😐 ☹
I can factorise an algebraic expression by taking out common factors	☺ 😐 ☹	☺ 😐 ☹	☺ 😐 ☹
I can multiply two expressions	☺ 😐 ☹	☺ 😐 ☹	☺ 😐 ☹
I can factorise $x^2 + bx + c$	☺ 😐 ☹	☺ 😐 ☹	☺ 😐 ☹
I can simplify an algebraic expression	☺ 😐 ☹	☺ 😐 ☹	☺ 😐 ☹
I can rearrange an algebraic expression to change the subject	☺ 😐 ☹	☺ 😐 ☹	☺ 😐 ☹
I can use and manipulate surds	☺ 😐 ☹	☺ 😐 ☹	☺ 😐 ☹
I can use the laws of indices	☺ 😐 ☹	☺ 😐 ☹	☺ 😐 ☹
I can use functions	☺ 😐 ☹	☺ 😐 ☹	☺ 😐 ☹
I can plot and determine coordinate from a graph	☺ 😐 ☹	☺ 😐 ☹	☺ 😐 ☹
I can plot a line from the expression $y = mx + c$	☺ 😐 ☹	☺ 😐 ☹	☺ 😐 ☹
I can identify parallel lines from the expression $y = mx + c$	☺ 😐 ☹	☺ 😐 ☹	☺ 😐 ☹
I can determine the expression $y = mx + c$ from a graph	☺ 😐 ☹	☺ 😐 ☹	☺ 😐 ☹
I can find the gradient of a line	☺ 😐 ☹	☺ 😐 ☹	☺ 😐 ☹
I can find the intercept of a line	☺ 😐 ☹	☺ 😐 ☹	☺ 😐 ☹
I can identify roots from a graph	☺ 😐 ☹	☺ 😐 ☹	☺ 😐 ☹
I can identify intercepts from a graph	☺ 😐 ☹	☺ 😐 ☹	☺ 😐 ☹

Primrose Kitten – YouTube Tutorials for Science and Maths.

I can identify turning points from a graph	☺ 😐 ☹	☺ 😐 ☹	☺ 😐 ☹
I can recognise and sketch the graphs for linear functions	☺ 😐 ☹	☺ 😐 ☹	☺ 😐 ☹
I can recognise and sketch the graphs for quadratic functions	☺ 😐 ☹	☺ 😐 ☹	☺ 😐 ☹
I can recognise and sketch the graphs for cubic functions	☺ 😐 ☹	☺ 😐 ☹	☺ 😐 ☹
I can recognise and sketch the graphs for $\frac{1}{x}$	☺ 😐 ☹	☺ 😐 ☹	☺ 😐 ☹
I can plot graphs	☺ 😐 ☹	☺ 😐 ☹	☺ 😐 ☹
I can interpret distance-time graphs	☺ 😐 ☹	☺ 😐 ☹	☺ 😐 ☹
I can interpret velocity-time graphs	☺ 😐 ☹	☺ 😐 ☹	☺ 😐 ☹
I can solve an equation	☺ 😐 ☹	☺ 😐 ☹	☺ 😐 ☹
I can find approximate solutions to an equation from a graph	☺ 😐 ☹	☺ 😐 ☹	☺ 😐 ☹
I can solve quadratic equations by factorising	☺ 😐 ☹	☺ 😐 ☹	☺ 😐 ☹
I can solve two simultaneous equations	☺ 😐 ☹	☺ 😐 ☹	☺ 😐 ☹
I can make equations from a situation given in text	☺ 😐 ☹	☺ 😐 ☹	☺ 😐 ☹
I can solve linear inequalities and show the answer on a number line	☺ 😐 ☹	☺ 😐 ☹	☺ 😐 ☹
I can find terms in a sequence from the nth term	☺ 😐 ☹	☺ 😐 ☹	☺ 😐 ☹
I can find the nth term from a sequence	☺ 😐 ☹	☺ 😐 ☹	☺ 😐 ☹
I can recognise and use square numbers	☺ 😐 ☹	☺ 😐 ☹	☺ 😐 ☹
I can recognise and use cube numbers	☺ 😐 ☹	☺ 😐 ☹	☺ 😐 ☹
I can recognise and use triangular numbers	☺ 😐 ☹	☺ 😐 ☹	☺ 😐 ☹
Higher tier only			
I can simplify algebraic expression involving fractions	☺ 😐 ☹	☺ 😐 ☹	☺ 😐 ☹
I can factorise quadratic equations ($ax^2 + bx + c$)	☺ 😐 ☹	☺ 😐 ☹	☺ 😐 ☹
I can use algebra to construct proofs	☺ 😐 ☹	☺ 😐 ☹	☺ 😐 ☹
I can interpret inverse functions	☺ 😐 ☹	☺ 😐 ☹	☺ 😐 ☹
I can interpret composite functions	☺ 😐 ☹	☺ 😐 ☹	☺ 😐 ☹
I can identify perpendicular line from a graph	☺ 😐 ☹	☺ 😐 ☹	☺ 😐 ☹
I can identify turning points on a graph by completing the square	☺ 😐 ☹	☺ 😐 ☹	☺ 😐 ☹
I can recognise, sketch and interpret graphs for exponential functions	☺ 😐 ☹	☺ 😐 ☹	☺ 😐 ☹
I can recognise, sketch and interpret graphs for trigonometric functions (sin, cos and tan)	☺ 😐 ☹	☺ 😐 ☹	☺ 😐 ☹
I can sketch translations of a functions	☺ 😐 ☹	☺ 😐 ☹	☺ 😐 ☹
I can sketch transformations of a function	☺ 😐 ☹	☺ 😐 ☹	☺ 😐 ☹
I can plot and interpret exponential graphs	☺ 😐 ☹	☺ 😐 ☹	☺ 😐 ☹
I can calculate and estimate the gradients of graphs	☺ 😐 ☹	☺ 😐 ☹	☺ 😐 ☹
I can calculate and estimate the area under a graph	☺ 😐 ☹	☺ 😐 ☹	☺ 😐 ☹
I can determine distance from a distance time graph	☺ 😐 ☹	☺ 😐 ☹	☺ 😐 ☹

I can determine speed from a distance time graph	☺ 😐 ☹	☺ 😐 ☹	☺ 😐 ☹
I can determine distance from a velocity time graph	☺ 😐 ☹	☺ 😐 ☹	☺ 😐 ☹
I can determine speed from a velocity time graph	☺ 😐 ☹	☺ 😐 ☹	☺ 😐 ☹
I can use the equation of a circle to find the equation of a tangent	☺ 😐 ☹	☺ 😐 ☹	☺ 😐 ☹
I can solve quadratic equations be completing the square	☺ 😐 ☹	☺ 😐 ☹	☺ 😐 ☹
I can find approximate solutions to an equation using iteration	☺ 😐 ☹	☺ 😐 ☹	☺ 😐 ☹
I can solve linear inequalities using a graph	☺ 😐 ☹	☺ 😐 ☹	☺ 😐 ☹
I can find the nth term for quadratic sequences	☺ 😐 ☹	☺ 😐 ☹	☺ 😐 ☹

Ratio, Proportion and Rates of Change Learning Objectives

Specification statement	Self-assessment		
These are the bits the exam board wants you to know, make sure you can do all of these...	First review 4-7 months before exam	Second review 1-2 months before exam	Final review Week before exam
I can recall and convert standard units for time	☺ 😐 ☹	☺ 😐 ☹	☺ 😐 ☹
I can recall and convert standard units for length	☺ 😐 ☹	☺ 😐 ☹	☺ 😐 ☹
I can recall and convert standard units for area	☺ 😐 ☹	☺ 😐 ☹	☺ 😐 ☹
I can recall and convert standard units for volume	☺ 😐 ☹	☺ 😐 ☹	☺ 😐 ☹
I can recall and convert standard units for mass	☺ 😐 ☹	☺ 😐 ☹	☺ 😐 ☹
I can recall and convert standard units for speed	☺ 😐 ☹	☺ 😐 ☹	☺ 😐 ☹
I can recall and convert standard units for rates of pay	☺ 😐 ☹	☺ 😐 ☹	☺ 😐 ☹
I can recall and convert standard units for prices	☺ 😐 ☹	☺ 😐 ☹	☺ 😐 ☹
I can recall and convert standard units for density	☺ 😐 ☹	☺ 😐 ☹	☺ 😐 ☹
I can recall and convert standard units for pressure	☺ 😐 ☹	☺ 😐 ☹	☺ 😐 ☹
I can interpret and use scale factors	☺ 😐 ☹	☺ 😐 ☹	☺ 😐 ☹
I can interpret and use scale diagrams	☺ 😐 ☹	☺ 😐 ☹	☺ 😐 ☹
I can interpret and use maps	☺ 😐 ☹	☺ 😐 ☹	☺ 😐 ☹
I can interpret and use ratio notation	☺ 😐 ☹	☺ 😐 ☹	☺ 😐 ☹
I can apply ratio to real life context	☺ 😐 ☹	☺ 😐 ☹	☺ 😐 ☹
I can express a relationship as a ratio	☺ 😐 ☹	☺ 😐 ☹	☺ 😐 ☹
I can use parts to work out ratios	☺ 😐 ☹	☺ 😐 ☹	☺ 😐 ☹
I can link ratios to fractions	☺ 😐 ☹	☺ 😐 ☹	☺ 😐 ☹
I can use and interpret percentages	☺ 😐 ☹	☺ 😐 ☹	☺ 😐 ☹
I can calculate percentage change	☺ 😐 ☹	☺ 😐 ☹	☺ 😐 ☹
I can compare two things using percentages	☺ 😐 ☹	☺ 😐 ☹	☺ 😐 ☹
I can calculate interest	☺ 😐 ☹	☺ 😐 ☹	☺ 😐 ☹
I can solve questions that involve direct proportionality	☺ 😐 ☹	☺ 😐 ☹	☺ 😐 ☹
I can solve questions that involve inverse proportionality	☺ 😐 ☹	☺ 😐 ☹	☺ 😐 ☹
I can compare different quantities using rations	☺ 😐 ☹	☺ 😐 ☹	☺ 😐 ☹
I can recall that x being inversely proportional to Y is the same as x being proportional to $\frac{1}{y}$	☺ 😐 ☹	☺ 😐 ☹	☺ 😐 ☹
I can use equations to show direct and inverse proportion	☺ 😐 ☹	☺ 😐 ☹	☺ 😐 ☹
I can recognise direct and inverse proportion on a graph	☺ 😐 ☹	☺ 😐 ☹	☺ 😐 ☹

Primrose Kitten – YouTube Tutorials for Science and Maths.

I can recall that the gradient of a line shows the rate of change	☺ 😐 ☹	☺ 😐 ☹	☺ 😐 ☹
I can calculate compound interest	☺ 😐 ☹	☺ 😐 ☹	☺ 😐 ☹
Higher tier only	☺ 😐 ☹	☺ 😐 ☹	☺ 😐 ☹
I can use a tangent to find the gradient at a point on a line	☺ 😐 ☹	☺ 😐 ☹	☺ 😐 ☹
I can determine rate of change from a gradient	☺ 😐 ☹	☺ 😐 ☹	☺ 😐 ☹
I can use iteration	☺ 😐 ☹	☺ 😐 ☹	☺ 😐 ☹

Geometry and Measures Learning Objectives

Specification statement These are the bits the exam board wants you to know, make sure you can do all of these...	Self-assessment		
	First review 4-7 months before exam	Second review 1-2 months before exam	Final review Week before exam
I can define the term point	☺ ☐ ☹	☺ ☐ ☹	☺ ☐ ☹
I can define the term line	☺ ☐ ☹	☺ ☐ ☹	☺ ☐ ☹
I can define the term vertices	☺ ☐ ☹	☺ ☐ ☹	☺ ☐ ☹
I can define the term edge	☺ ☐ ☹	☺ ☐ ☹	☺ ☐ ☹
I can define the term plane	☺ ☐ ☹	☺ ☐ ☹	☺ ☐ ☹
I can define the term parallel lines	☺ ☐ ☹	☺ ☐ ☹	☺ ☐ ☹
I can define the term perpendicular lines	☺ ☐ ☹	☺ ☐ ☹	☺ ☐ ☹
I can define the term right angles	☺ ☐ ☹	☺ ☐ ☹	☺ ☐ ☹
I can define the term polygons	☺ ☐ ☹	☺ ☐ ☹	☺ ☐ ☹
I can define the term regular polygon	☺ ☐ ☹	☺ ☐ ☹	☺ ☐ ☹
I can define the term reflection	☺ ☐ ☹	☺ ☐ ☹	☺ ☐ ☹
I can define the term rotational symmetry	☺ ☐ ☹	☺ ☐ ☹	☺ ☐ ☹
I can use a ruler and compass to draw the perpendicular bisect of a line	☺ ☐ ☹	☺ ☐ ☹	☺ ☐ ☹
I can use a ruler and compass to solve loci problems	☺ ☐ ☹	☺ ☐ ☹	☺ ☐ ☹
I can recall the rules of angles to find angles at a point	☺ ☐ ☹	☺ ☐ ☹	☺ ☐ ☹
I can recall the rules of angles to find angles on a straight line	☺ ☐ ☹	☺ ☐ ☹	☺ ☐ ☹
I can recall the rules of angles to find vertically opposite angles	☺ ☐ ☹	☺ ☐ ☹	☺ ☐ ☹
I can recall the rules of angles to find corresponding angles on parallel lines (do not call them Z angles)	☺ ☐ ☹	☺ ☐ ☹	☺ ☐ ☹
I can recall the rules of angles to find the sum of angles in a triangle	☺ ☐ ☹	☺ ☐ ☹	☺ ☐ ☹
I can recall and apply the properties of a square	☺ ☐ ☹	☺ ☐ ☹	☺ ☐ ☹
I can recall and apply the properties of a rectangle	☺ ☐ ☹	☺ ☐ ☹	☺ ☐ ☹
I can recall and apply the properties of a parallelogram	☺ ☐ ☹	☺ ☐ ☹	☺ ☐ ☹
I can recall and apply the properties of a trapezium	☺ ☐ ☹	☺ ☐ ☹	☺ ☐ ☹
I can recall and apply the properties of a kite	☺ ☐ ☹	☺ ☐ ☹	☺ ☐ ☹
I can recall and apply the properties of a rhombus	☺ ☐ ☹	☺ ☐ ☹	☺ ☐ ☹

I can recall and apply the rules of congruence triangles (SSS, SAS, ASA, and RHS)	☺ ☺ ☹	☺ ☺ ☹	☺ ☺ ☹
I can recall and apply the properties of an equilateral triangle	☺ ☺ ☹	☺ ☺ ☹	☺ ☺ ☹
I can recall and apply the properties of an isosceles triangle	☺ ☺ ☹	☺ ☺ ☹	☺ ☺ ☹
I can rotate a shape	☺ ☺ ☹	☺ ☺ ☹	☺ ☺ ☹
I can reflect a shape	☺ ☺ ☹	☺ ☺ ☹	☺ ☺ ☹
I can translate a shape	☺ ☺ ☹	☺ ☺ ☹	☺ ☺ ☹
I can enlarge a shape	☺ ☺ ☹	☺ ☺ ☹	☺ ☺ ☹
I can define the term centre of a circle	☺ ☺ ☹	☺ ☺ ☹	☺ ☺ ☹
I can define the term radius	☺ ☺ ☹	☺ ☺ ☹	☺ ☺ ☹
I can define the term chord	☺ ☺ ☹	☺ ☺ ☹	☺ ☺ ☹
I can define the term diameter	☺ ☺ ☹	☺ ☺ ☹	☺ ☺ ☹
I can define the term circumference	☺ ☺ ☹	☺ ☺ ☹	☺ ☺ ☹
I can define the term tangent	☺ ☺ ☹	☺ ☺ ☹	☺ ☺ ☹
I can define the term arc	☺ ☺ ☹	☺ ☺ ☹	☺ ☺ ☹
I can define the term sector	☺ ☺ ☹	☺ ☺ ☹	☺ ☺ ☹
I can define the term segment	☺ ☺ ☹	☺ ☺ ☹	☺ ☺ ☹
I can identify properties (including; faces, edges, surfaces and vertices) of cubes	☺ ☺ ☹	☺ ☺ ☹	☺ ☺ ☹
I can identify properties (including; faces, edges, surfaces and vertices) of cuboids	☺ ☺ ☹	☺ ☺ ☹	☺ ☺ ☹
I can identify properties (including; faces, edges, surfaces and vertices) of prisms	☺ ☺ ☹	☺ ☺ ☹	☺ ☺ ☹
I can identify properties (including; faces, edges, surfaces and vertices) of cylinders	☺ ☺ ☹	☺ ☺ ☹	☺ ☺ ☹
I can identify properties (including; faces, edges, surfaces and vertices) of pyramids	☺ ☺ ☹	☺ ☺ ☹	☺ ☺ ☹
I can identify properties (including; faces, edges, surfaces and vertices) of cones	☺ ☺ ☹	☺ ☺ ☹	☺ ☺ ☹
I can identify properties (including; faces, edges, surfaces and vertices) of spheres	☺ ☺ ☹	☺ ☺ ☹	☺ ☺ ☹
I can convert a 2D shape in to a 3D shape and a 3D shape into a 2D shape	☺ ☺ ☹	☺ ☺ ☹	☺ ☺ ☹
I can measure lines and angles	☺ ☺ ☹	☺ ☺ ☹	☺ ☺ ☹
I can measure lines on a map and use scale conversions	☺ ☺ ☹	☺ ☺ ☹	☺ ☺ ☹
I can use bearings	☺ ☺ ☹	☺ ☺ ☹	☺ ☺ ☹
I can recall and use how to find the area of a triangle	☺ ☺ ☹	☺ ☺ ☹	☺ ☺ ☹

Primrose Kitten – YouTube Tutorials for Science and Maths.

Flashcards to help with this are available on www.primrosekitten.com			
I can recall and use how to find the area of a parallelogram	☺ 😐 ☹	☺ 😐 ☹	☺ 😐 ☹
I can recall and use how to find the area of a trapezium	☺ 😐 ☹	☺ 😐 ☹	☺ 😐 ☹
I can recall and use how to find the volume of a cuboid	☺ 😐 ☹	☺ 😐 ☹	☺ 😐 ☹
I can recall and use how to find the volume of a cylinder	☺ 😐 ☹	☺ 😐 ☹	☺ 😐 ☹
I can recall the formulae to determine the circumference of a circle	☺ 😐 ☹	☺ 😐 ☹	☺ 😐 ☹
I can recall the formulae to determine the area of a circle	☺ 😐 ☹	☺ 😐 ☹	☺ 😐 ☹
I can recall the formulae to determine the perimeter of a 2D shape	☺ 😐 ☹	☺ 😐 ☹	☺ 😐 ☹
I can recall the formulae to determine the surface area of a sphere	☺ 😐 ☹	☺ 😐 ☹	☺ 😐 ☹
I can recall the formulae to determine the volume of sphere	☺ 😐 ☹	☺ 😐 ☹	☺ 😐 ☹
I can recall the formulae to determine the surface area of a pyramid	☺ 😐 ☹	☺ 😐 ☹	☺ 😐 ☹
I can recall the formulae to determine the volume of a pyramid	☺ 😐 ☹	☺ 😐 ☹	☺ 😐 ☹
I can recall the formulae to determine the surface area of a cone	☺ 😐 ☹	☺ 😐 ☹	☺ 😐 ☹
I can recall the formulae to determine the volume of a cone	☺ 😐 ☹	☺ 😐 ☹	☺ 😐 ☹
I can calculate arc lengths	☺ 😐 ☹	☺ 😐 ☹	☺ 😐 ☹
I can calculate angles in a circle	☺ 😐 ☹	☺ 😐 ☹	☺ 😐 ☹
I can calculate sectors of a circle	☺ 😐 ☹	☺ 😐 ☹	☺ 😐 ☹
I can determine relationships in similar shapes	☺ 😐 ☹	☺ 😐 ☹	☺ 😐 ☹
I can recall and apply the formula for Pythagoras $a^2 + b^2 = c^2$	☺ 😐 ☹	☺ 😐 ☹	☺ 😐 ☹
I can recall and apply the formula for the trigonometric ratios (sin, cos, tan)	☺ 😐 ☹	☺ 😐 ☹	☺ 😐 ☹
I can recall the exact values of sin θ and cos θ where θ = 0°, 30°, 45°, 60° and 90°; and know the exact value of tan θ where θ = 0°, 30°, 45° and 60° **Flashcards to help with this are available on www.primrosekitten.com**	☺ 😐 ☹	☺ 😐 ☹	☺ 😐 ☹
I can describe a translation as a vector	☺ 😐 ☹	☺ 😐 ☹	☺ 😐 ☹
I can add vectors	☺ 😐 ☹	☺ 😐 ☹	☺ 😐 ☹
I can subtract vectors	☺ 😐 ☹	☺ 😐 ☹	☺ 😐 ☹
I can multiply vectors	☺ 😐 ☹	☺ 😐 ☹	☺ 😐 ☹
Higher tier only			

I can enlarge a shape by a negative factor	☺ 😐 ☹	☺ 😐 ☹	☺ 😐 ☹
I can describe a combinations of rotations, reflections and translations	☺ 😐 ☹	☺ 😐 ☹	☺ 😐 ☹
I can apply circle theorem	☺ 😐 ☹	☺ 😐 ☹	☺ 😐 ☹
I can prove circle theorem	☺ 😐 ☹	☺ 😐 ☹	☺ 😐 ☹
I can recall and apply $\frac{a}{\sin A} = \frac{b}{\sin B} = \frac{c}{\sin C}$	☺ 😐 ☹	☺ 😐 ☹	☺ 😐 ☹
I can recall and apply $a^2 = b^2 + c^2 - 2bc \sin C$	☺ 😐 ☹	☺ 😐 ☹	☺ 😐 ☹
I can recall and apply area of a non-right angled triangle = $\frac{1}{2}$ ab sin C	☺ 😐 ☹	☺ 😐 ☹	☺ 😐 ☹

Probability Learning Objectives

Specification statement These are the bits the exam board wants you to know, make sure you can do all of these…	Self-assessment		
	First review 4-7 months before exam	Second review 1-2 months before exam	Final review Week before exam
I can describe the probability of an event from a table or tree	☺ ☐ ☹	☺ ☐ ☹	☺ ☐ ☹
I can determine if an event if fair, random or equally likely	☺ ☐ ☹	☺ ☐ ☹	☺ ☐ ☹
I can give a value (out of 1) to the probability of an event	☺ ☐ ☹	☺ ☐ ☹	☺ ☐ ☹
I can recall that total probability must equal 1	☺ ☐ ☹	☺ ☐ ☹	☺ ☐ ☹
I can combine sets of probability data using tables	☺ ☐ ☹	☺ ☐ ☹	☺ ☐ ☹
I can combine sets of probability data using Venn diagrams	☺ ☐ ☹	☺ ☐ ☹	☺ ☐ ☹
I can combine sets of probability data using trees	☺ ☐ ☹	☺ ☐ ☹	☺ ☐ ☹
I can combine sets of probability data using grids	☺ ☐ ☹	☺ ☐ ☹	☺ ☐ ☹
I can calculate the probability of a combination of independent events	☺ ☐ ☹	☺ ☐ ☹	☺ ☐ ☹
I can calculate the probability of a combination of dependent events	☺ ☐ ☹	☺ ☐ ☹	☺ ☐ ☹
Higher tier only			
I can calculate conditional probability	☺ ☐ ☹	☺ ☐ ☹	☺ ☐ ☹

Statistics Learning Objectives

Specification statement These are the bits the exam board wants you to know, make sure you can do all of these...	Self-assessment		
	First review 4-7 months before exam	Second review 1-2 months before exam	Final review Week before exam
I can determine the properties of a population or distribution from a sample	☺ 😐 ☹	☺ 😐 ☹	☺ 😐 ☹
I can interpret, construct and use frequency tables	☺ 😐 ☹	☺ 😐 ☹	☺ 😐 ☹
I can interpret, construct and use bar charts	☺ 😐 ☹	☺ 😐 ☹	☺ 😐 ☹
I can interpret, construct and use pie charts	☺ 😐 ☹	☺ 😐 ☹	☺ 😐 ☹
I can interpret, construct and use pictograms	☺ 😐 ☹	☺ 😐 ☹	☺ 😐 ☹
I can interpret, construct and use line charts	☺ 😐 ☹	☺ 😐 ☹	☺ 😐 ☹
I can compare sets of data from graphs	☺ 😐 ☹	☺ 😐 ☹	☺ 😐 ☹
I can calculate the median	☺ 😐 ☹	☺ 😐 ☹	☺ 😐 ☹
I can calculate the mode	☺ 😐 ☹	☺ 😐 ☹	☺ 😐 ☹
I can calculate the mean	☺ 😐 ☹	☺ 😐 ☹	☺ 😐 ☹
I can calculate the range	☺ 😐 ☹	☺ 😐 ☹	☺ 😐 ☹
I can calculate the modal class	☺ 😐 ☹	☺ 😐 ☹	☺ 😐 ☹
I can apply statistic to a population	☺ 😐 ☹	☺ 😐 ☹	☺ 😐 ☹
I can interpret scatter graphs	☺ 😐 ☹	☺ 😐 ☹	☺ 😐 ☹
I can recognise correlation	☺ 😐 ☹	☺ 😐 ☹	☺ 😐 ☹
I can draw a line of best fit	☺ 😐 ☹	☺ 😐 ☹	☺ 😐 ☹
I can make predictions from data	☺ 😐 ☹	☺ 😐 ☹	☺ 😐 ☹
I can work out future trends	☺ 😐 ☹	☺ 😐 ☹	☺ 😐 ☹
Higher tier only			
I can construct and interpret histograms with equal and unequal class intervals	☺ 😐 ☹	☺ 😐 ☹	☺ 😐 ☹
I can construct and interpret box plots	☺ 😐 ☹	☺ 😐 ☹	☺ 😐 ☹
I can determine quartiles and inter-quartiles ranges	☺ 😐 ☹	☺ 😐 ☹	☺ 😐 ☹

15% Number

#1 Number – Surds. Non-calculator

Fully worked video explanation at; https://youtu.be/AAZK1b-QtH0

Simplify the following ...

$\sqrt{3^0} + \sqrt{3^1} + \sqrt{3^2} + \sqrt{3^3} + \sqrt{3^4}$

#2 Number – Estimation. Non-calculator

Fully worked video explanation at; https://youtu.be/8f3Mzy7Pr8E

A cylinder of liquid strontium has a density of 6.98 g/cm^3, the cylinder has a radius of 5.2cm and a height of 0.1975m. Find the mass in kg.

#3 Number – Writing recurring decimal as fractions. Non-calculator

Fully worked video explanation at; https://youtu.be/OZBNRR-bb14
Flashcards to help with this are available on www.primrosekitten.com

Write the following as a fraction.

$11.\dot{3}$

$14.8\dot{3}$

$21.\dot{3}$

#4 Number – Writing fractions as recurring decimals. Non-calculator.

Fully worked video explanation at; https://youtu.be/XMkUf9tUW9s
Flashcards to help with this are available on www.primrosekitten.com

Write the following as decimal.

$\frac{29}{9} + \frac{4}{3}$

$\frac{2}{11} + \frac{5}{12}$

$\frac{5}{6} + \frac{7}{9}$

#5 Number – Standard form. Non- calculator.

Fully worked video explanation at; https://youtu.be/aKYMuQP87HI

If a 3.72×10^{29} kN force is exerted over an area that is 2.74×10^{14} cm by 3.93×10^{21} cm, what is the pressure in Pascals"?

#6 Number – Surds. Non-calculator

Fully worked video explanation at; https://youtu.be/Twbh7_T6UQ4

Rewrite the following in its simplest terms.

$(\sqrt{18} \times \sqrt{6}) + \sqrt{675} + \frac{12}{\sqrt{3}}$

#7 Number- Upper and Lower bounds.

Fully worked video explanation at; https://youtu.be/uhIToc5WvnI

For the equation $x = \frac{z}{\sqrt{y}+z}$ where $y = 2.89$ and $z = 1.97 \times 10^{-3}$ (both numbers are given to 3 significant figures), find the upper and lower bounds of x.

#8 Number - Product rule for counting. Non-calculator.

Fully worked video explanation at; https://youtu.be/8gIbLdhrFWM

An odd numbered 6-digit code is generated. The 4th and 5th digit are prime numbers, the 3rd number is even, the second number is a factor of 22. Find the total number of possible combinations.

20% Ratio, Proportion and Rate of Change

#9 Ratio, Proportion and Rate of Change – Iteration

Fully worked video explanation at; https://youtu.be/8QjQ9Islz6M

Find a solution to the equation $2x^2 - 6x + 1 = 0$, correct to 3dp

#10 Ratio, Proportion and Rate of Change – Ratio

Fully worked video explanation at; https://youtu.be/I1T26V4vXaQ

Two similar cuboids are compared. The smaller on has a height of 4.1cm, the larger of has a volume 216 times that of the smaller one. What is the height of the larger cuboid?

#11 Ratio, Proportion and Rate of Change. Changing Ratio.

Fully worked video explanation at; https://youtu.be/HECc6ryOYJE

My sons toy box is full of dinosaurs and cars. The chance of him pulling out a toy and it being a dinosaur is 4/9. After much 'discussion' I remove a one legged T.Rex, a Stegosaurs with no tail and a Pterodactyl covered in paint. The chance of him now picking a car is 2/3. How many dinosaurs and cars were there originally?

#12 Ratio, Proportion and Rate of Change. Percentages. Non-calculator.

Fully worked video explanation at; https://youtu.be/efShir_Mq2w

In a fruit bowl 30% of the fruit are bananas, 60% of the bananas are unripe and 50% of the rest is unripe. What overall percentage is unripe?

#13 Ratio, Proportion and Rate of Change. Inverse proportion

Fully worked video explanation at; https://youtu.be/XpXRLUSQfYY

α is inversely proportional to $\beta 2$, when α = 100, β = 20. Find α when β = 25

#14 Ratio, Proportion and Rate of Change. Compound Interest.

Fully worked video explanation at; https://youtu.be/oTyTGRVxIq0

Neesha earnt £7.75 an hour working over the summer holidays. She worked at a local soft play centre making tea and coffee for exhausted mums. Over the course of the summer she worked 15 hours a week for 7 weeks, apart from the week she went to V-festival where she only worked 8 hours. At the end of the summer she had saved up all the money and decided to invest it for 3 years. Interest on this account was paid every three months at a rate of 2.45%. how much money did she have at the end?

#15 Ratio, Proportion and Rate of Change. Iteration

Fully worked video explanation at; https://youtu.be/MV8acgPjOjc

Use trial and improvement to solve x^3 + 4x = 67, to 1 decimal place.

#16 Ratio, Proportion and Rate of Change. Rate of change.

Fully worked video explanation at; https://youtu.be/7J18dNy31QI

Compare the rate of change at 20 seconds and 200 seconds

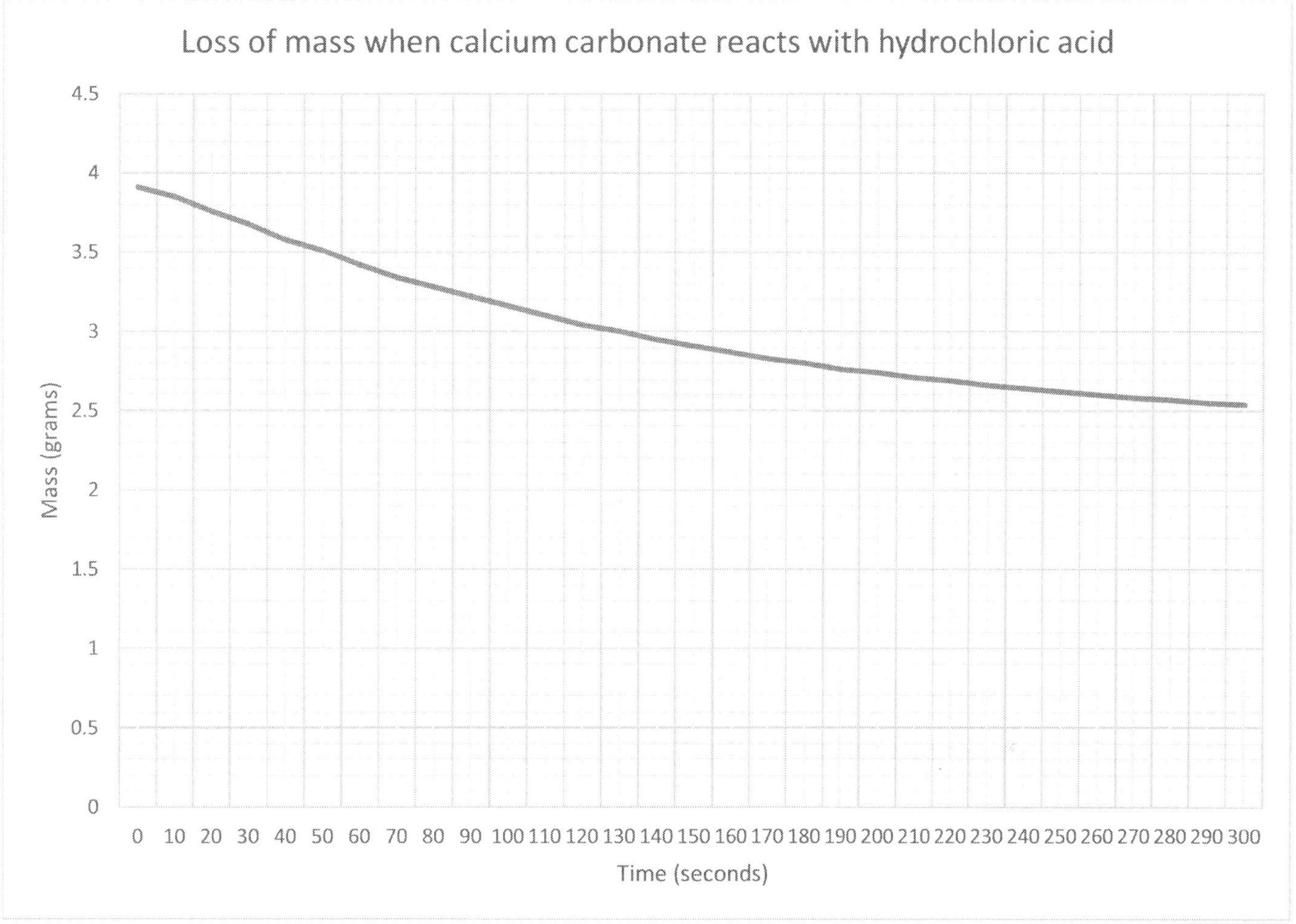

#17 Ratio, Proportion and Rate of Change. Unit Conversions

Fully worked video explanation at; https://youtu.be/fHhRNpmDtL0

Convert the quantities and units on the left to those on the right.

58 cm^3	...............m^3
98 cm^3	...............m^3
6.7 m^3	............cm^3
43 m^3	............cm^3
2 days	.... seconds
6 days	.... seconds
450 seconds	.... days
1290 seconds	.... days
15 meters/second	..........kilometres/hour
89 meters/second	..........kilometres/hour
27 kilometres/hour	.... meters/second
5 kilometres/hour	.... meters/second
576 g	............tonnes
156 g	............tonnes
6.9 tonnes	...........g
8.4 tonnes	...........g
56 g/cm^3	........kg/m^3
7 g/cm^3	........kg/m^3
4 kg/m^3	.... g/cm^3
15 kg/m^3	.... g/cm^3

#18 Ratio, Proportion and Rate of Change. Rates.

Fully worked video explanation at; https://youtu.be/IdZyIuBYqsU

Over the summer holiday two classes of students are set homework. The first class works in groups of five and spend four days working on the project, from 10am until 6pm. The second class worked from ten am until three pm, and worked in larger groups of seven. How many days did it take the second class to complete the homework?

30% Algebra

#19 Algebra – Indices.

Fully worked video explanation at; https://youtu.be/95TF57npvlM

Simplify the following …

$x^{\frac{1}{2}}(25xy^2)^{\frac{1}{2}}$

$y^4(2xy^2z^3)^3$

$x^6(25x^6y^{10}z^4)^{\frac{1}{2}}$

$x^2(27x^3y^6z)^{1/3}$

#20 Algebra – Indices. Non-calculator.

Fully worked video explanation at; https://youtu.be/GmrW6_rfi3M

Simplify the following ….

$64^{2/3}$

$81^{3/2}$

$625^{\frac{3}{4}}$

$81^{\frac{3}{4}}$

#21 Algebra – Changing the subject of a formula

Fully worked video explanation at; https://youtu.be/NmT8RrRW6dA

Make a the subject

$$3a^3 = \frac{(b^{\frac{1}{2}}c^{-3}a)^2}{c^{-5}}$$

#22 Algebra – Algebraic fractions

Fully worked video explanation at; https://youtu.be/lX-ree59ODw

Simplify the following…

$$\frac{4x^2 - 16}{3x^2 - 6x} \times \frac{x^2 + 3x}{x^2 + 10x + 21}$$

#23 Algebra – Algebraic fractions

Fully worked video explanation at; https://youtu.be/eDay73-L7t8

Simplify the following …

$$\frac{x^2 - 2x - 15}{5x + 15} \div \frac{3x - 12}{x^2 - 16x}$$

#24 Algebra – Composite functions

Fully worked video explanation at; https://youtu.be/8vXkRr4WZOc

Find c, if $fgh(x) \equiv ax^2 + abx - 3x + 3b + c$

$f(x) = 3x + 2$
$g(x) = x^2 + 1$
$h(x) = x - 1$

Primrose Kitten – YouTube Tutorials for Science and Maths.

#25 Algebra – Composite functions

Fully worked video explanation at; https://youtu.be/BDa4e0AWS-A

Find c, if $fhg(x) \equiv a(x-4)(x+4) + ab\sqrt{20x} + 2b + 9c$

$f(x) = 3x - 7$
$g(x) = x + \sqrt{5}$
$h(x) = x^2$

#26 Algebra – Quadratic nth term

Fully worked video explanation at; https://youtu.be/WCd1y1764m4

Find the nth term for the following sequence…

1   3   9   19   33

#27 Algebra – Solving a quadratic equation

Fully worked video explanation at; https://youtu.be/fayKU6UWFks

Find the two solutions for the following equation…

$$\frac{4x+1}{x+4} - \frac{x+1}{x-3} = 1 - 6x$$

#28 Algebra - Using the equation of a circle to find the equation of a tangent

Fully worked video explanation at; https://youtu.be/qyC_qxYrz7Q

A circle has the $x^2 + y^2 = 34$ and a centre at 0, 0. A tangent touches the circle at point 5, -3, what is the equation of the tangent.

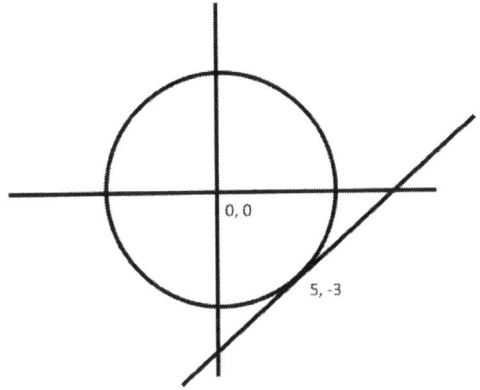

#29 Algebra – Velocity time graphs. Non-calculator.

Fully worked video explanation at; https://youtu.be/aUl_KQ-mg4s

The graph shows a journey that covered 175m. The velocity was constant at v m/s for 5 seconds and the journey ended at 2v m/s. Find the value for v

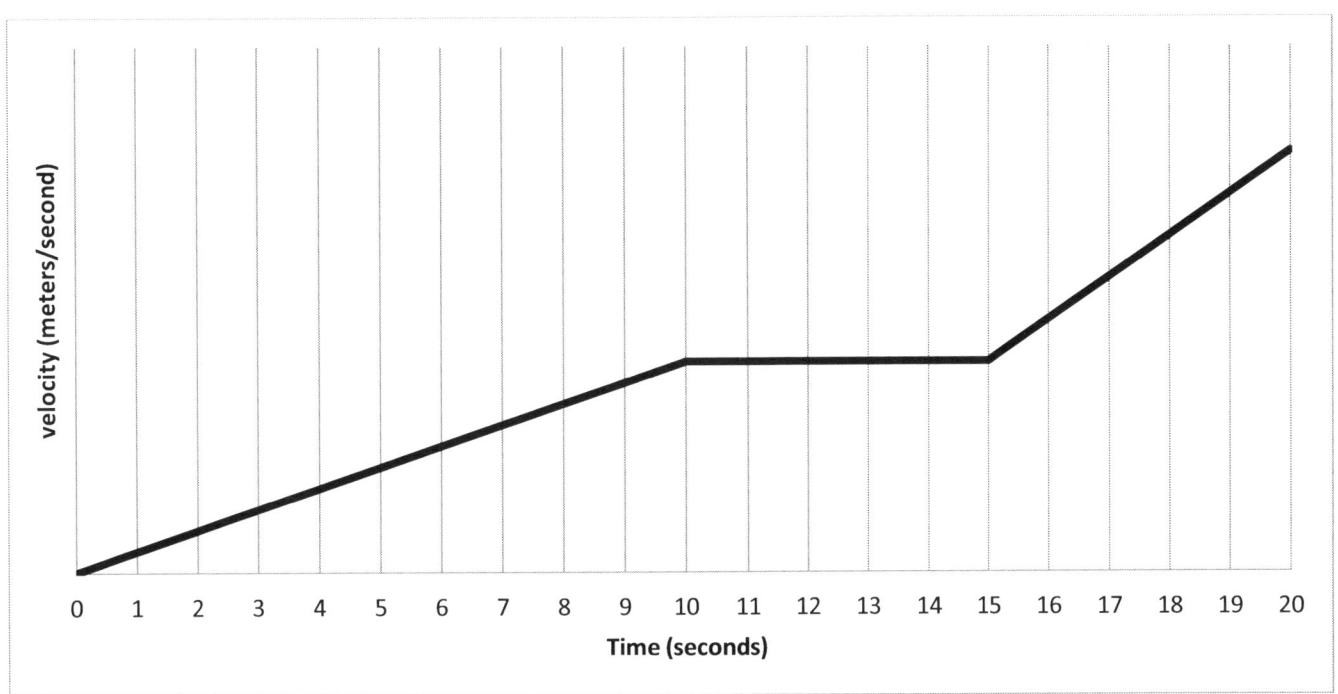

#30 Algebra. Quadratic Graphs.

Fully worked video explanation at; https://youtu.be/pxQHhqPFrKo

Sketch the graphs for…

$y = x^2$
$y = -x^2$
$y = 2x^2$
$y = \frac{1}{2}x^2$
$y = x^2 + 3$
$y = x^2 - 5$
$y = (x - 3)^2$
$y = (x + 5)^2$
$y = (x - 4)^2 + 3$

#31 Algebra. Cubic Graphs.

Fully worked video explanation at; https://youtu.be/Wys1BfNCBnw

Sketch the graphs for…

$y = x^3$
$y = -x^3$
$y = x^3 + 3$
$y = (x - 3)^3$
$y = \frac{1}{2}x^3$
$y = 3x^3$
$y = 2x^3 + 6$

#32 Algebra. Exponential and Reciprocal Graphs

Fully worked video explanation at; https://youtu.be/Ae01NkOvc08

Sketch the following graphs...

$y = -2^x$
$y = 2^{-x}$
$y = 3/x$

#33 Algebra. Proof.

Fully worked video explanation at; https://youtu.be/zi3wqM6DZK8

Use algebra to prove that $(n+1)^2 - (n-1)^2 + 1$ is always going to be odd when n is a positive value.

15% Statistics and Probability

#34 Statistics and Probability – Venn Diagrams

Fully worked video explanation at; https://youtu.be/2Tpp53NfoGk

Draw a Venn diagram for the following information.

I have a rather extensive shoe collection; I picked a selection of 31 pairs, in that section were 11 pink shoes, 13 with glitter and bows on (3 are fabulous and have pink, glittery, bows!) 1 pair is plain black suede with a tiny bow, 16 in total have bows, 5 are pink with glitter.

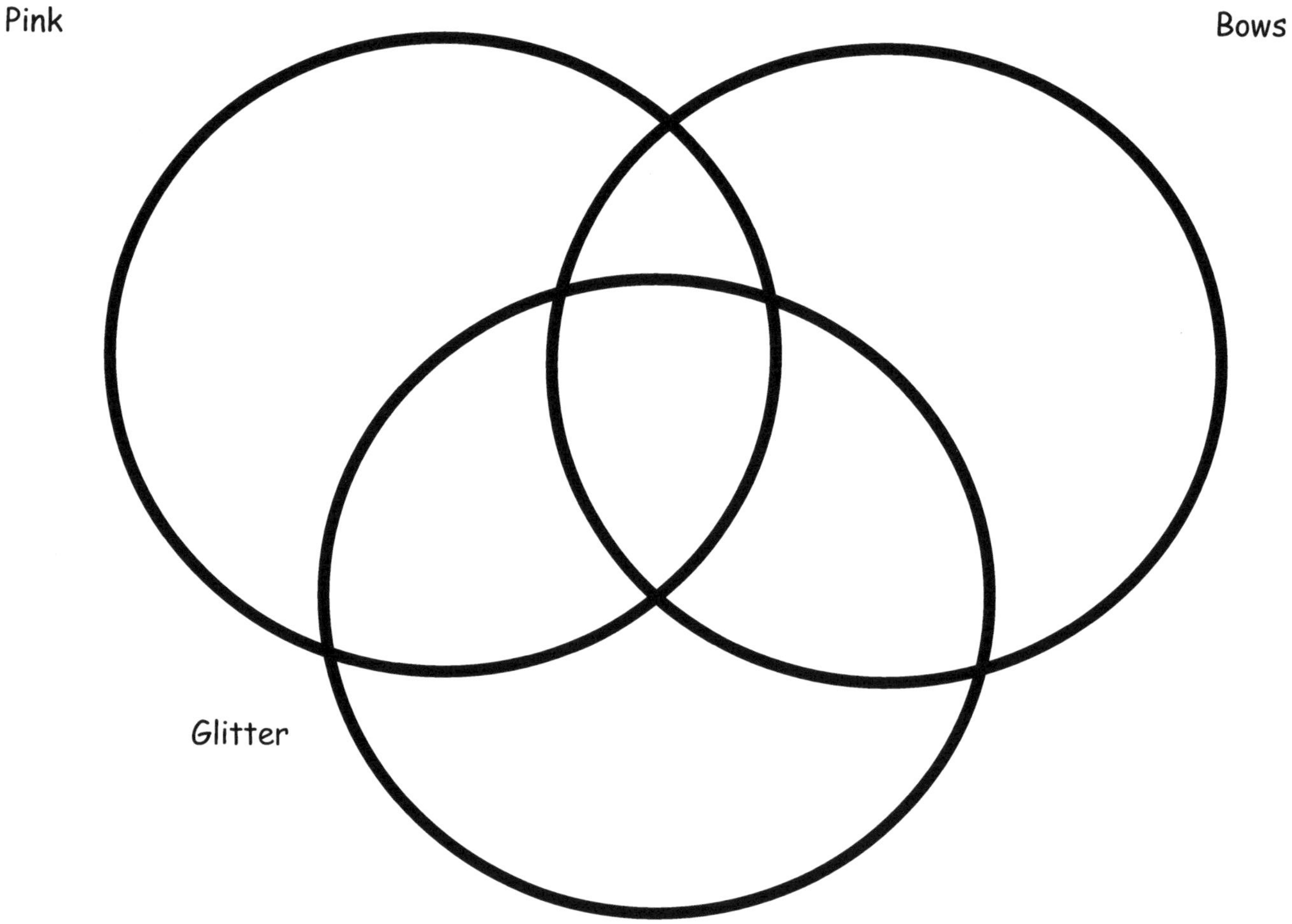

Pink

Bows

Glitter

#35 Statistics and Probability - Probability

Fully worked video explanation at; https://youtu.be/pyidwpprjsg

In a pencil case, there are a range of different coloured pens. That chances of picking out two pens that are the same colour are 53/141. If red, blue and black pens are in a 1;2;3 ratio; how many red pens are in the case?

#36 Statistics and Probability. Venn Diagrams.

Fully worked video explanation at; https://youtu.be/xDu39a_oVUw

Sketch the following diagrams;

$P(A \cap B)$

$P(A \cup B)$

$P(A' \cap B')$

$P(A \cup B')$

#37 Statistics and Probability. Box plots.

Fully worked video explanation at; https://youtu.be/dF_rM2bYiBE

At a family reunion, a survey of ages was taken, great uncle Erik was the oldest at 96 years old (there is a lovely photo of him holding a tiny new-born baby). The interquartile range of ages was 32 years with the median being 49. The upper quartile age was 61.

Draw a box plot to represent this data.

#38 Statistics and Probability. Histograms.

Fully worked video explanation at; https://youtu.be/8RMafiSlVuU

Draw the graph for the data below.

Velocity (m/s)	Frequency
$1 < v \leq 5$	8
$5 < v \leq 7$	6
$7 < v \leq 11$	4
$11 < v \leq 20$	18
$20 < v \leq 30$	10

#39 Statistics and Probability. Conditional Probability.

Fully worked video explanation at; https://youtu.be/nFUgaekjQqo

A GCSE had two papers, only 25% of a class passed both papers and 45% of this class passed the first paper. What percent of those students who passed the first paper also passed the second?

#40 Statistics and Probability. Mean.

Fully worked video explanation at; https://youtu.be/tHvG66KtFoI

A teacher had a league table of test results displayed on her wall. After 9 tests the Logan's mean score was 77, after 10 tests his score was 76. What did he score on his last test?

20% Geometry and Measure

#41 Geometry and Measure – Trigonometry and Surds. Non-calculator.

Fully worked video explanation at; https://youtu.be/GTHpRp8Pmdo
Flashcards to help with learning your accurate values for trigonometry are available on www.primrosekitten.com

Show the two triangles are similar

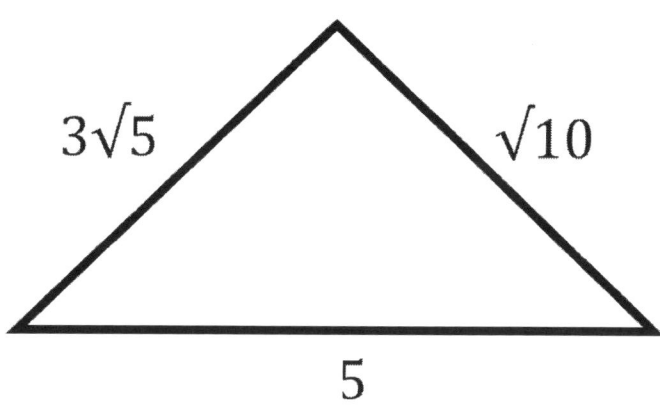

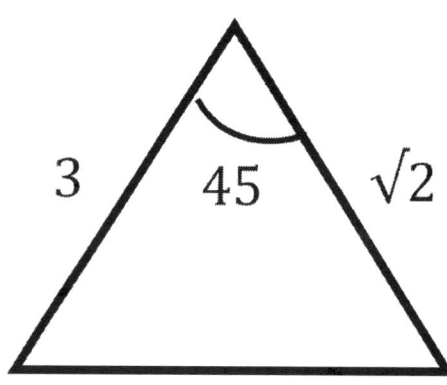

#42 Geometry and Measure – Bearings

Fully worked video explanation at; https://youtu.be/z9oGfYug3KU

A ship leaves port and travels due north 10 miles to point A; at point A, the ship changes direction with a bearing of 48°. After travelling 5 miles (and reaching point B) the bearing is again changed, the ship sets off the 7 miles to point C on a bearing of 192°. What is the distance between point A and C?

Primrose Kitten – YouTube Tutorials for Science and Maths.

#43 Geometry and Measure – Trigonometry and Pythagoras

Fully worked video explanation at; ttps://youtu.be/9PxgOgFzcUs

The composite shape below is made up from two triangles and a square. Angles A:B:C are in a 1:2:5 ratio and angles E:F:G are in a 1:2:3 ratio. Find side y.

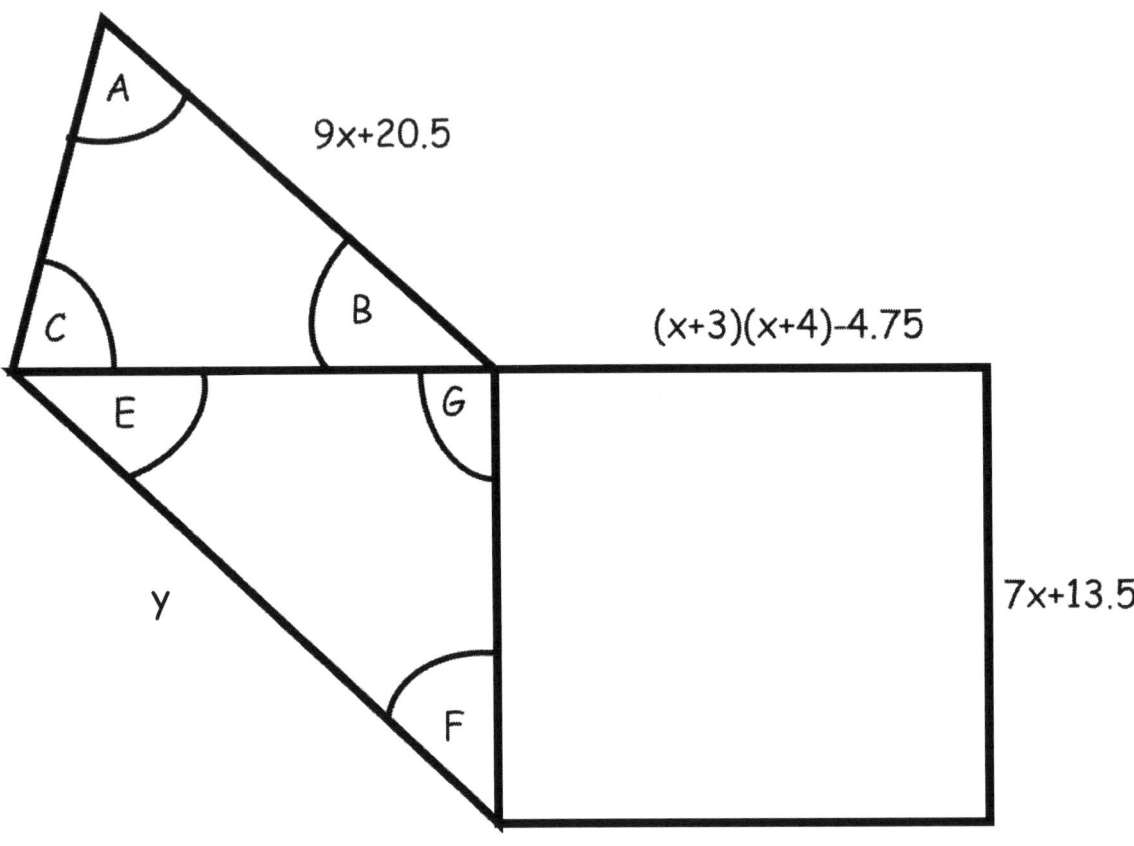

#44 Geometry and Measure – Vectors

Fully worked video explanation at; https://youtu.be/aPtnWRo6v5Y

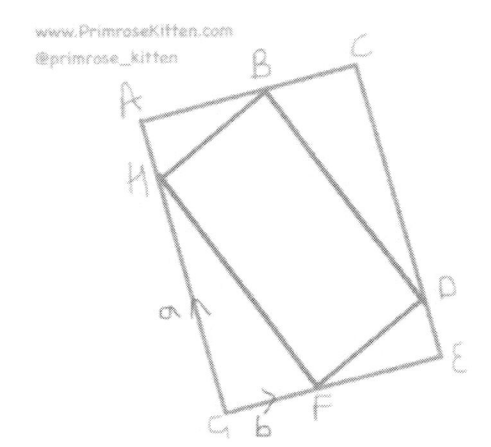

ACEG is a parallelogram, if AB=3BC, CD=3DE, EF=3FG and GH=3HA, prove that BDFH is also a parallelogram.

#45 Geometry and Measure – Spheres and Cones

Fully worked video explanation at; https://youtu.be/Wct9Pw8-j9k

A sphere with a radius of 9cm, is 4/7th full, the water is transferred into a cone. The depth of the water is 8cm. What is the radius of water sitting in the cone?

#46 Geometry and Measure. Circle Theorem.

Fully worked video explanation at; https://youtu.be/Iglwi4CHfUU

Find the angle at ABC.

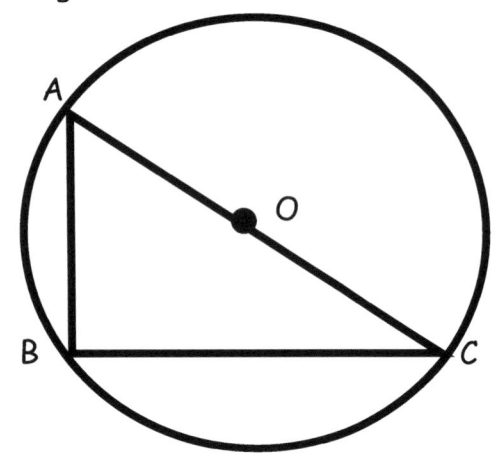

#47 Geometry and Measure. Enlargement.

Fully worked video explanation at; https://youtu.be/OzCxZIdgrWY

Redraw the shape below enlarged through the point 1,2 with a scale factor of -2.

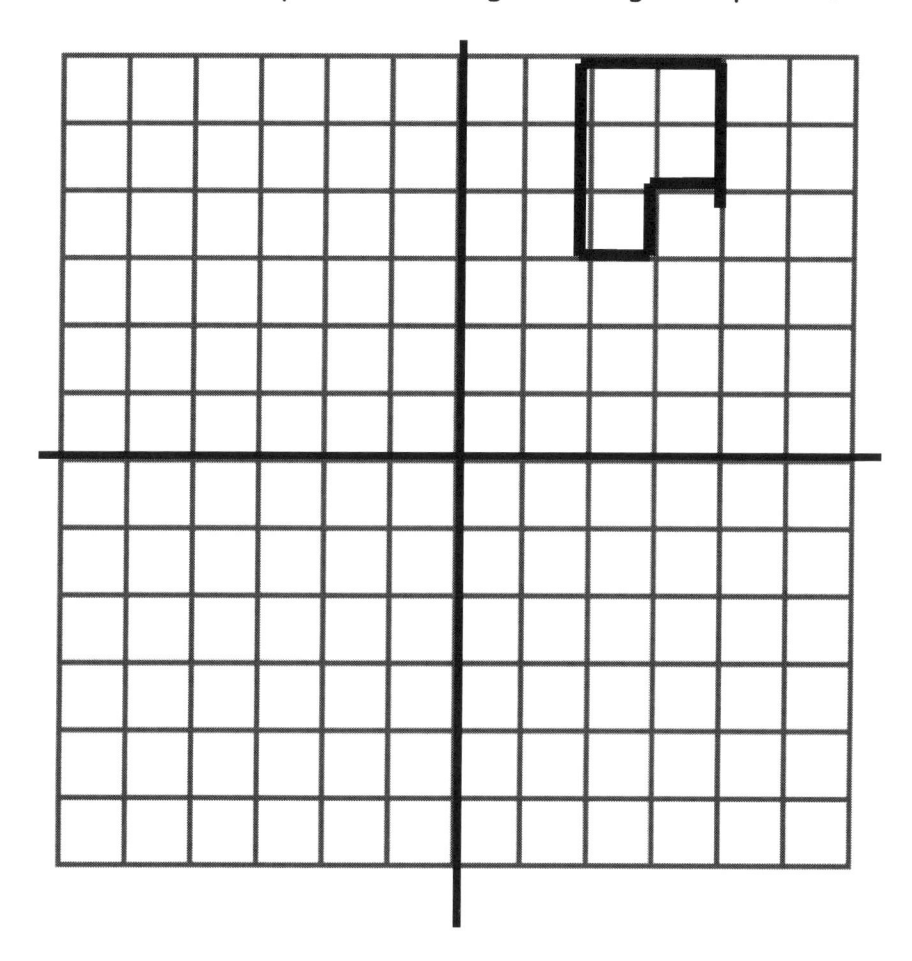

#48 Geometry and Measure. 3D Pythagoras. Non-calculator.

Fully worked video explanation at; https://youtu.be/Zwise1DzurY

A large cuboid has a side of 3cm, 4cm and 12cm, work out the length of the long diagonal.

#49 Geometry and Measure. Area of a Triangle.

Fully worked video explanation at; https://youtu.be/-I1zrp4CUQY

A triangle has sides of 4cm, 5cm and 7cm. Find the area of this triangle.

#50 Geometry and Measure. Trigonometry. Non-calculator

Fully worked video explanation at; https://youtu.be/u6sjj9me4M8
Flashcards to help with learning your accurate values for trigonometry are available on www.primrosekitten.com

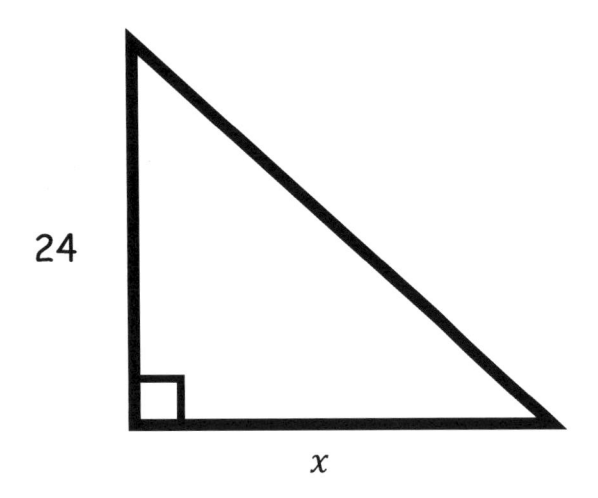

The two triangles have the same area, find x.

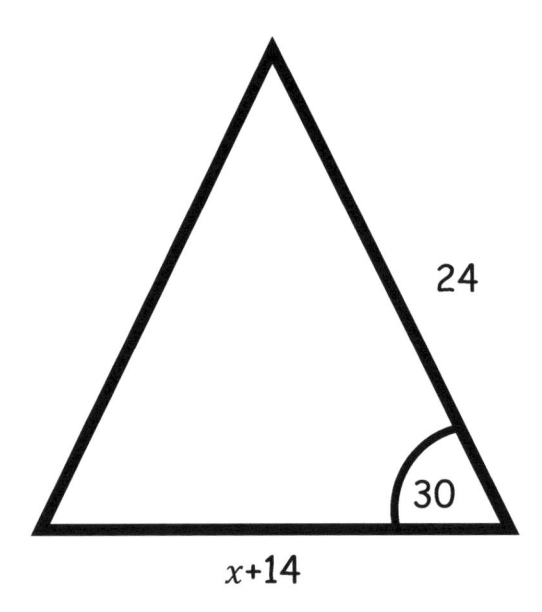

Algebra Book 2

#1
Express as a single fraction
$$\frac{x+1}{x^2+x-6} + \frac{2x}{x^2-7x+10}$$

https://youtu.be/1zD7Z-EDzno

#2
Express as a single fraction
$$\frac{3x+1}{x^2+4x+3} - \frac{2x+8}{x^2+5x+4}$$

https://youtu.be/QFoivu5mMfU

#3
Rationalise the denominator and simplify fully.
$$\frac{6-7\sqrt{3}}{8+5\sqrt{3}}$$

https://youtu.be/S8jWZX6bS9s

#4
Factorise fully
$$12x^2 - 14x - 10$$

https://youtu.be/THLic7tGO90

#5
Factorise fully
$$8x^2 + 2x - 3$$

https://youtu.be/Exg4BRToMKM

#6
Simplify
$$x^{\frac{1}{3}}(8x^2y^6)^{\frac{1}{3}}$$

https://youtu.be/9NNoPMJ4Mno

#7
Simplify
$$\sqrt{\frac{x^2 \times 25x^{\frac{1}{3}}}{64x}}$$

https://youtu.be/gnh_KnGB8ds

Primrose Kitten – YouTube Tutorials for Science and Maths.

8
Find the nth term for the following sequence

$$4 \quad 9 \quad 18 \quad 31 \quad 48 \quad 69$$

https://youtu.be/n1Yla4OPlTE

9
Given that $fgh(x) \equiv 2ax^2 + abx + 3x + b + 2c$ find c

$f(x) = \dfrac{3x + 4}{2}$
$g(x) = x^2 + 5$
$h(x) = 2x - 3$

https://youtu.be/vguVY45kQv0

10
Make a the subject of the formula

$$2a^5 = \dfrac{(3a^2 b^{\frac{1}{2}} c^{-2})^2}{4c^{-7}}$$

https://youtu.be/UxvpqBUjc64

11
Make a the subject of the formula

$$5b^3 = \dfrac{2a + 3b^{-2}c}{7a - 4bc^{\frac{1}{2}}}$$

https://youtu.be/Tt6avA4xXx4

12
If the area of a triangle is $(11 + 5\sqrt{6})$ cm², and the height is $(3 - 2\sqrt{2})$ cm then find the length of the base

https://youtu.be/gsi7Yjmpokg

13

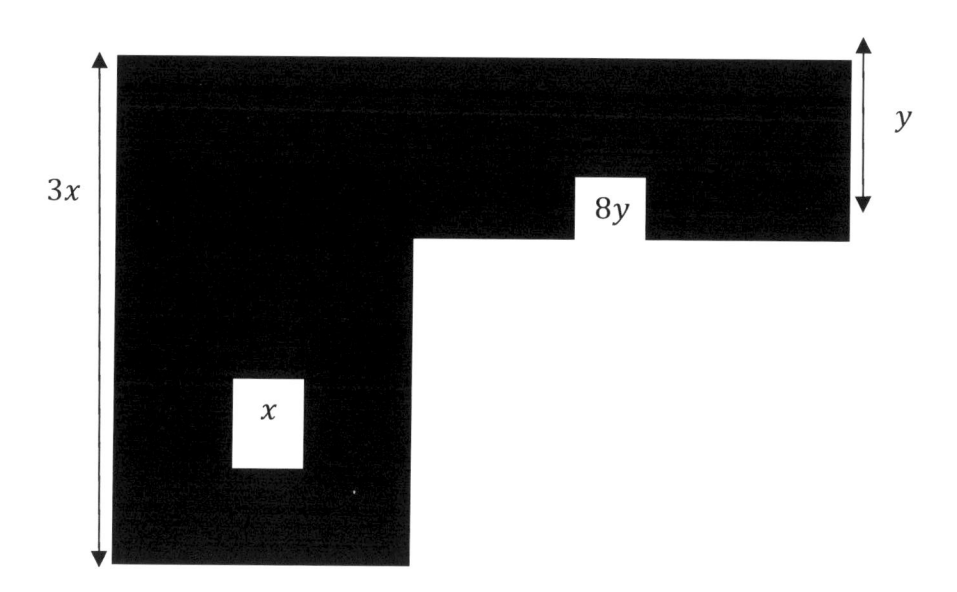

The perimeter of the shape is 40cm, the area of the shape is 30cm². Find values for x and y

14
Find $f^{-1}(x)$ if $f(x) = \sqrt{\dfrac{5x^2-3}{7}}$

15
Write $3x^2 - 7x + 15$ in the form $m(x+n)^2 + p$

16
Prove that the difference between the sum of two consecutive cube numbers and the difference between two consecutive cube numbers will always be an even number

17
Solve to find x
$$\dfrac{5x-3}{x+2} - \dfrac{2x+7}{x-1} = 2$$

18
Solve to find x
$$\dfrac{3x^2+7x+2}{2x-4} - \dfrac{4x+1}{2} = x-3$$

19

https://youtu.be/7O1AB4qbT08

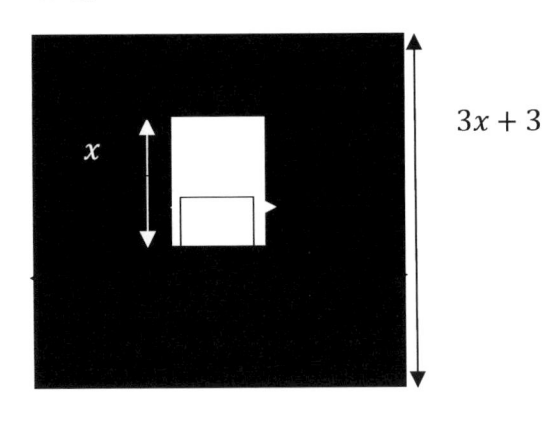

Here is a plan of a garden. The perimeter will be fencing and the shaded area will be grass. The fencing has a total length of 46m, and the grass will cover an area of 108m². Find the possible values for x and y

20

https://youtu.be/4vQFwsYC_Fs

Find $fhg(x)$
$f(x) = 2x^2 - 7x + 20$
$g(x) = x + 5$
$h(x) = 3x - 1$

21

https://youtu.be/DgrW6QDfYQY

Find the nth term for the following sequence...

3   7   21   51   103   183

22

https://youtu.be/YIAWZxg31to

Solve the inequality
$-2x^2 - 5x + 3 < 0$

23

https://youtu.be/druzZLixoao

Solve the inequality
$x^2 + 4x - 21 \leq 0$

24
https://youtu.be/EYGdvZ32h1Y

The graph for $f(x)$ is shown, sketch the graph for $-f(x + 3)$

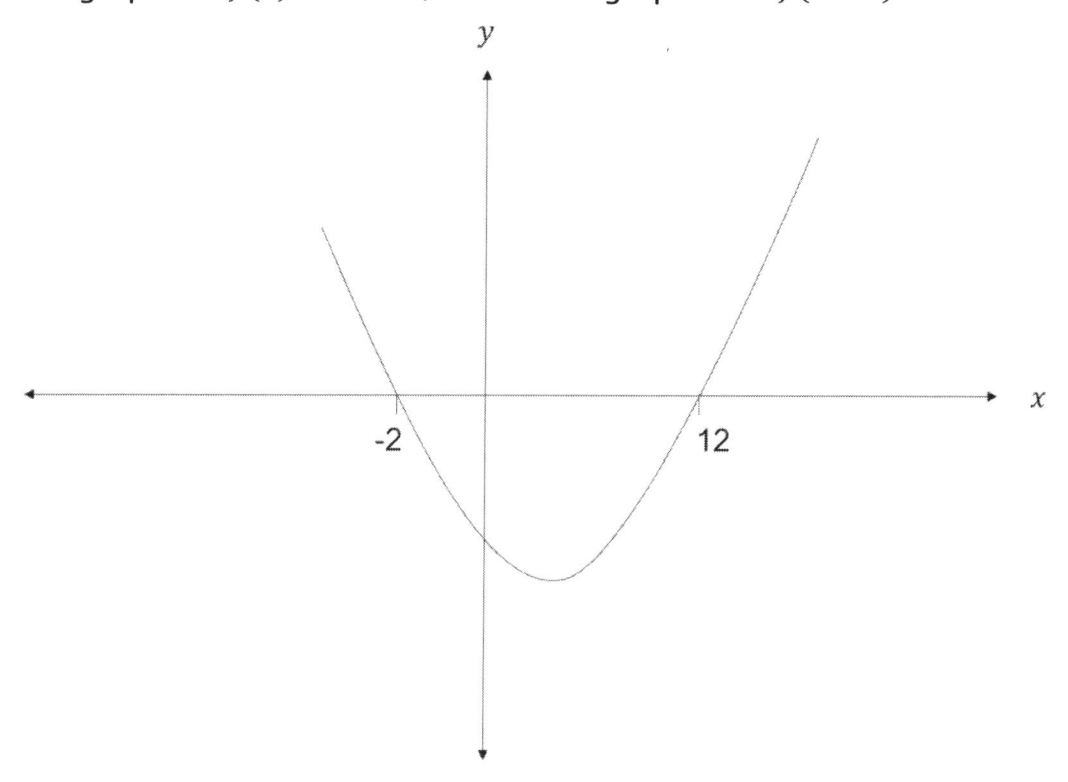

25
https://youtu.be/sxS4WhkwDMc

Sketch the graph of $y = x^2 - 7$

26
https://youtu.be/MKYGisag7R8

Sketch the graph of $y = (x + 2)^2$

27
https://youtu.be/3RBRjJfEKM4

Sketch the graph of $y = (x - 5)^2 + 1$

28
https://youtu.be/5jGqcgG6t8g

Sketch the graph of $y = -(x + 3)^2 + 9$

29
https://youtu.be/3JLZJMQfqZI

Sketch the graph of $y = \sin(x + 30)°$ for $-360 \leq x \leq 360$

30
https://youtu.be/37bM-2Qg_UQ

Sketch the graph of $y = \cos(x - 60)°$ for $-360 \leq x \leq 360$

31
Sketch the graph of $y = \sin(x-45)° + 2$ for $-360 \le x \le 360$

32
Given that $f(x) = \sqrt[3]{\dfrac{2x+5}{3x-7}}$ find $f^{-1}(x)$

33
Simplify $216^{\frac{2}{3}}$

no calculator!

34
Simplify $64^{\frac{4}{6}}$

no calculator!

35
Simplify $343^{\frac{2}{3}}$

no calculator!

36
A circle has the equation $x^2 + y^2 = 65$, a tangent touches the circle at point (7,4). What is the equation of the tangent?

37
Prove that the product of the squares of any two consecutive even numbers is always a multiple of 16.

38
Prove that the sum of three consecutive cube numbers is always a multiple of 3.

39
Given that a rectangle has a length of $(4\sqrt{5} - 2)$cm and an area of 12cm², find the height of the rectangle in its simplest form.

40
Simplify
$$\dfrac{x^2 + 4x - 21}{2x + 16} \times \dfrac{x^2 + 9x + 8}{x^2 - 8x + 15}$$

41
https://youtu.be/roALI76X5kA

Factorise
$6x^2 + 11x - 35$

42
https://youtu.be/vPSuBDSlXAE

Make e the subject of the formula

$t = \sqrt[3]{\dfrac{5e}{7} + 2a^2}$

43
https://youtu.be/0X8XiRmQYKA

Solve to find x
$12x^4 - 17x^3 - 7x^2 = 0$

44
https://youtu.be/B5kBjYEKq_M

A circle has the equation $(x - 3)^2 + (y - 1)^2 = 73$, a tangent touches the circle as point P (-5, 4). What is the equation of the tangent?

45
https://youtu.be/IaxV0oXfVd0

Given that $fgh(x) \equiv 6abx^2 - 3bcx + 2b$, find values for a, b and c.
$f(x) = (x + 1)^2$
$g(x) = 2x - 7$
$h(x) = 3x + 2$

46
https://youtu.be/wV0cQwqfbjE

Solve $3x^2 + 8x - 2 = 0$ by completing the square. Give your answer to two decimal places.

47
https://youtu.be/G97o-nTJbQE

Solve
$\dfrac{x^2 - 4}{x^2 + 6x + 5} \times \dfrac{x^2 - 6x - 7}{x + 2} = 3$

48

https://youtu.be/mMfFdNsBp64

The graph shows a journey that covered 195km, find the value for v

49

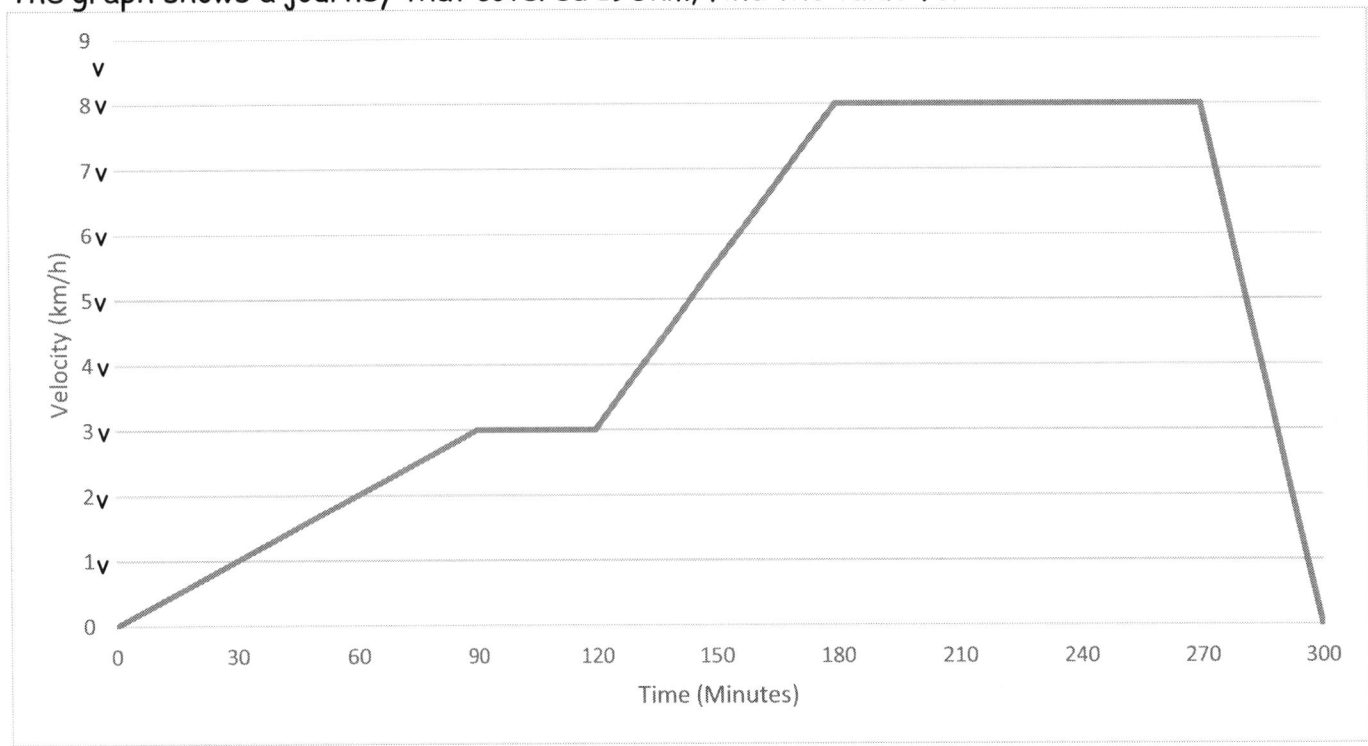

https://youtu.be/zgPFyd5qGzA

Prove algebraically that the sum of the squares of three consecutive odd numbers will always be odd.

50

https://youtu.be/-MJewOMjggg

Given that $f(x) = (\frac{7x-1}{2x+5})^2$ find $f^{-1}(4)$

Answers

#1 Number
$13 + 4\sqrt{3}$

#2 Number
10.5kg

#3 Number
34/3
89/6
64/3

#4 Number
$4.\dot{5}$
$0.59\dot{8}\dot{4}$
$1.6\dot{1}$

#5 Number
3.45Pa

#6 Number
$25\sqrt{3}$

#7 Number
upper= 1.16×10^{-3}
lower= 1.15×10^{-3}

#8 Number
8000

#9 Ratio, Proportion and Rate of Change
$x = 0.177$ and $x = 2.823$

#10 Ratio, Proportion and Rate of Change
24.6cm

#11 Ratio, Proportion and Rate of Change
8 dinosaurs and 10 cars

#12 Ratio, Proportion and Rate of Change
    53%

#13 Ratio, Proportion and Rate of Change
    64

#14 Ratio, Proportion and Rate of Change
    £1170.91

#15 Ratio, Proportion and Rate of Change
    3.7

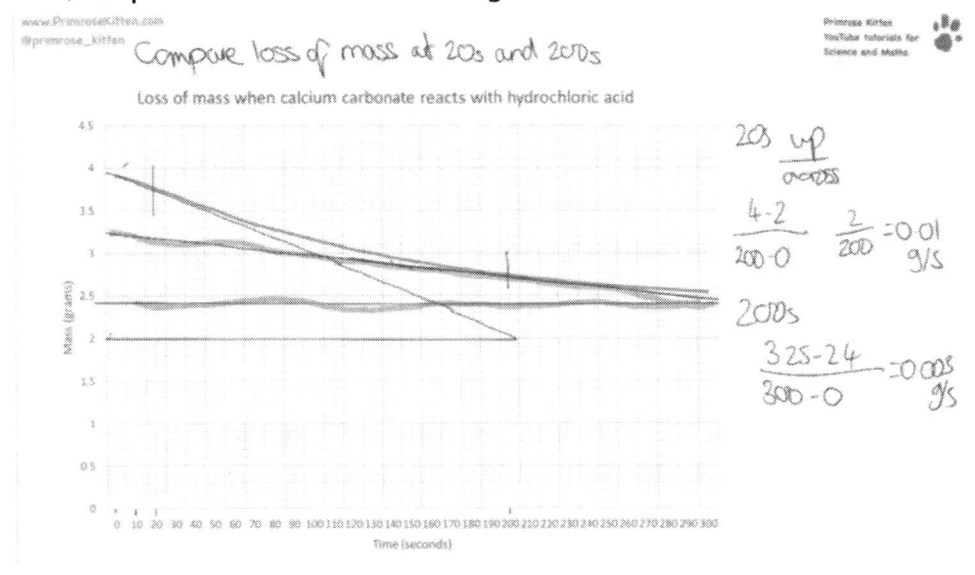

#16 Ratio, Proportion and Rate of Change

#17 Ratio, Proportion and Rate of Change

58 cm^3	0.0000 58 m^3
98 cm^3	0.000098 m^3
6.7 m^3	6700000 cm^3
43 m^3	43000000 cm^3
2 days	172800 seconds
6 days	518400 seconds

450 seconds	0.0052 days
1290 seconds	0.015 days
15 meters/second	54 kilometres/hour
89 meters/second	320.4 kilometres/hour
27 kilometres/hour	7.5 meters/second
5 kilometres/hour	1.4 meters/second
576 g	0.000576 tonnes
156 g	0.000156 tonnes
6.9 tonnes	6900000 g
8.4 tonnes	8400000 g
56 g/cm³	56000 kg/m³
7 g/cm³	7000 kg/m³
4 kg/m³	0.004 g/cm³
15 kg/m³	0.015 g/cm³

#18 Ratio, Proportion and Rate of Change
   4.6 days

#19 Algebra
   $5xy$
   $8x^3y^{10}z^9$
   $5x^9y^5z^2$
   $3x^3y^2z^{1/3}$

#20 Algebra
- 16
- 729
- 125
- 27

#21 Algebra
$$a = \frac{b}{3c}$$

#22 Algebra
$$\frac{4x(x+2)}{3x(x+7)}$$

#23 Algebra
$$\frac{(x-5)(x+4)}{15}$$

#24 Algebra
$C = 11$

#25 Algebra
$C = 6$

#26 Algebra
$2n^2 - 4n + 3$

#27 Algebra
$x = 4$ or $x = -2/3$

#28 Algebra
$y = 5/3\, x + -34/3$

#29 Algebra
10 m/s

#30 Algebra

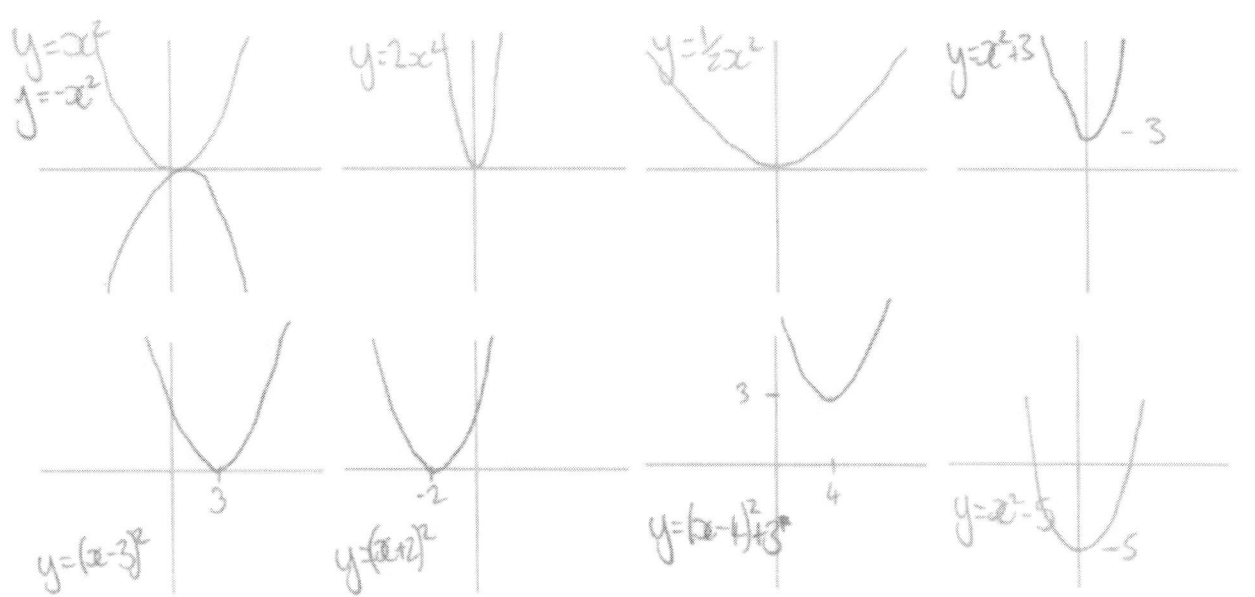

#31 Algebra

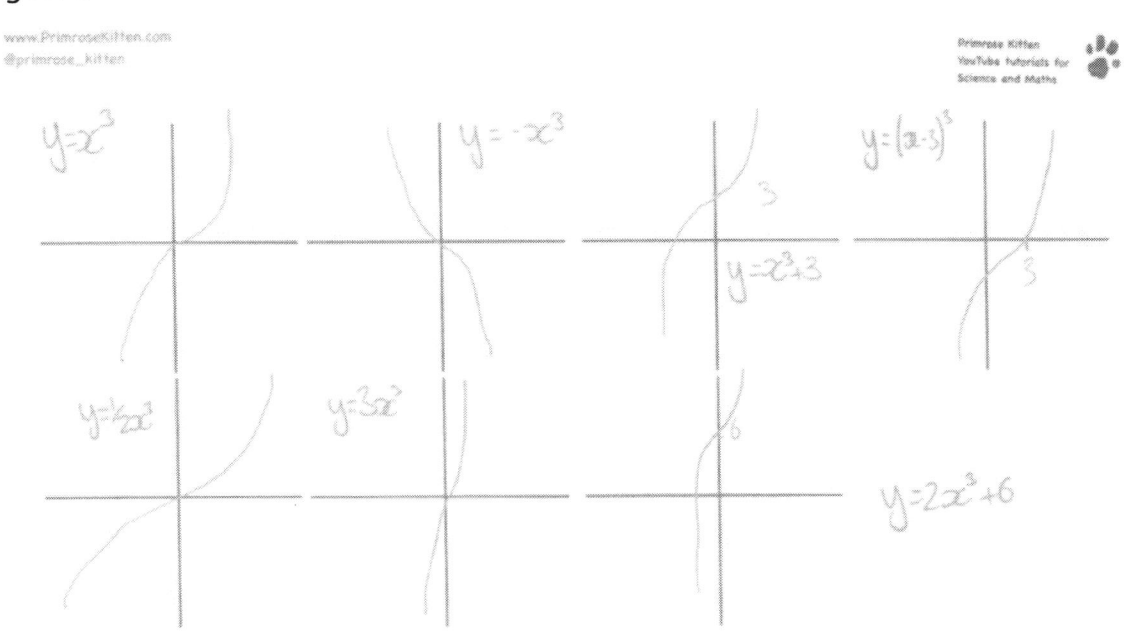

#32 Algebra

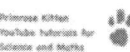

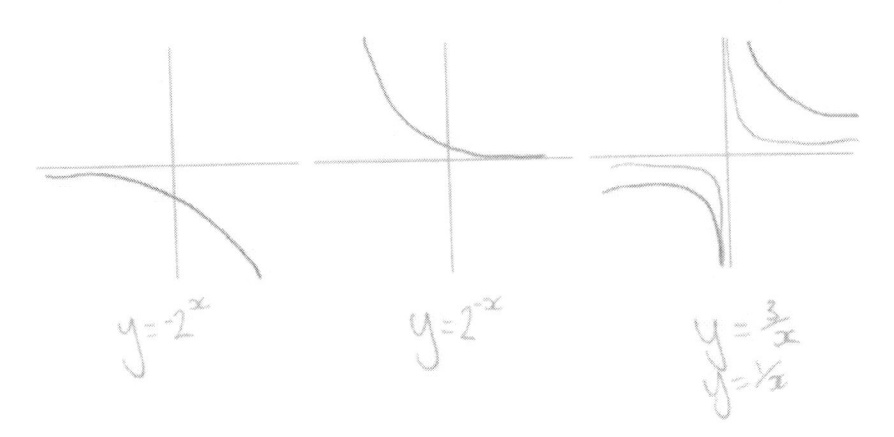

[Graphs: $y=-2^x$, $y=2^{-x}$, $y=\frac{3}{x}$, $y=\frac{1}{x}$]

#33 Algebra
    simplifies to 4n+1, 4n is even thus 4n+1 is odd

#34 Statistics and Probability

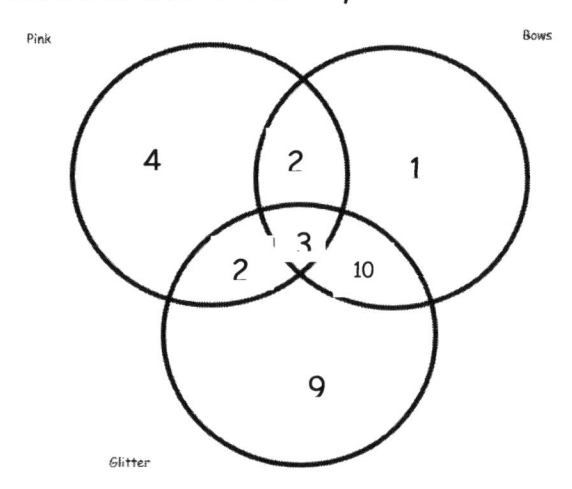

[Venn diagram — Pink: 4; Pink∩Bows: 2; Bows: 1; Pink∩Glitter: 2; Pink∩Bows∩Glitter: 3; Bows∩Glitter: 10; Glitter: 9]

#35 Statistics and Probability
    8 red pens

#36 Statistics and Probability

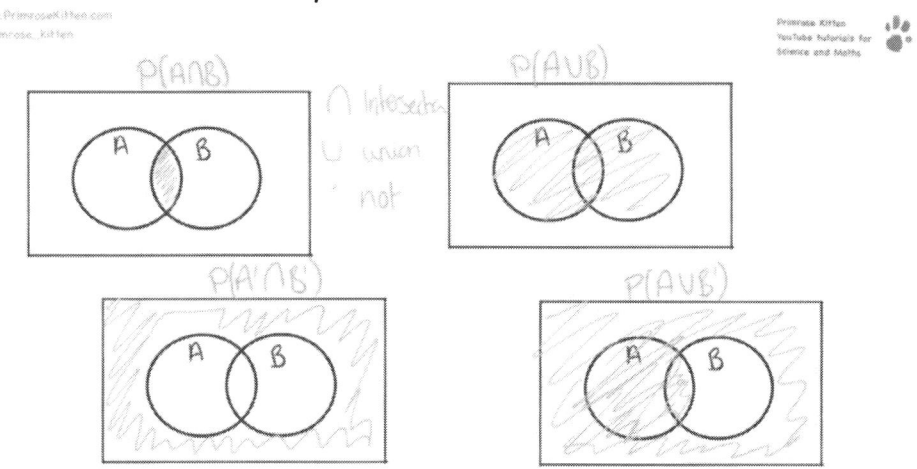

∩ Intersection
∪ Union
' not

#37 Statistics and Probability

At a family reunion, a survey of ages was taken, great uncle Erik was the oldest at 96 years old (there is a lovely photo of him holding a tiny new-born baby). The interquartile range of ages was 32 years with the median being 49. The upper quartile age was 61.

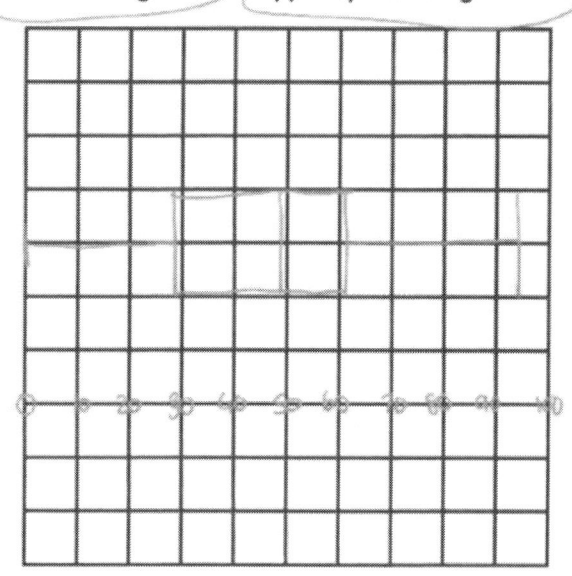

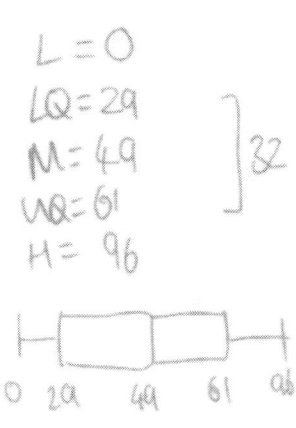

L = 0
LQ = 29
M = 49
UQ = 61   } 32
H = 96

0   29   49   61   96

#38 Statistics and Probability

Velocity (m/s)	Frequency	width	f.d.
1 < v ≤ 5	8	4	2
5 < v ≤ 7	6	2	3
7 < v ≤ 11	4	4	1
11 < v ≤ 20	18	9	2
20 < v ≤ 30	10	10	1

Frequency density = Frequency / class width

#39 Statistics and Probability
    56%

#40 Statistics and Probability
    67

#41 Geometry and Measure - Cosine Rule and Surds. Non-calculator.
    One triangle is √5 larger than the other

#42 Geometry and Measure
    4.17

#43 Geometry and Measure
    35.8

#44 Geometry and Measure
    HB and FD = 1/3a + 3b. FH and DB = a - b

#45 Geometry and Measure
    14.4

#46 Geometry and Measure
    90°

#47 Geometry and Measure

Redraw the shape below enlarged through the point 1,2 with a scale factor of -2.

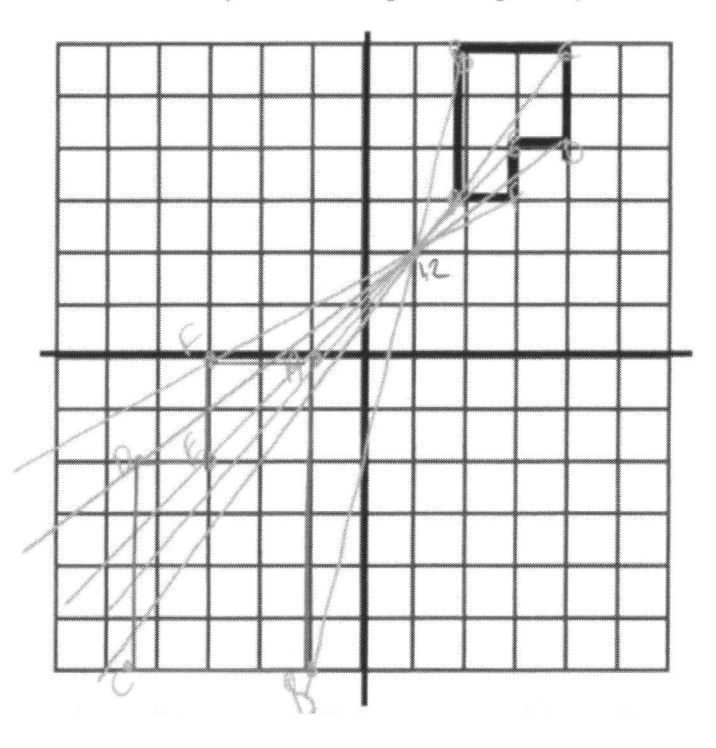

#48 Geometry and Measure
   13cm

#49 Geometry and Measure
   4.8cm

#50 Geometry and Measure
   14

Book 2 Answers
For full working and explanation see video links

Question	Answer
1	$\dfrac{3x^2 + 2x - 5}{(x+3)(x-2)(x-5)}$
2	$\dfrac{x-5}{(x+1)(x+3)}$
3	$-\dfrac{153 - 86\sqrt{3}}{11}$
4	$(6x - 10)(2x + 1)$
5	$(4x + 3)(2x - 1)$
6	$2xy^2$
7	$\dfrac{5}{8}x^{\frac{2}{3}}$
8	$2n^2 - n + 3$
9	$C = 15$
10	$a = \dfrac{9bc^3}{8}$

11	$$a = \dfrac{3b^{-2}c + 20b^4 c^{\frac{1}{2}}}{35b^3 - 2}$$
12	$$b = (66 + 44\sqrt{2} + 30\sqrt{6} + 20\sqrt{12})\,cm$$
13	$$x = 2,\ y = \dfrac{3}{2}$$
14	$$f^{-1}(x) = \sqrt{\dfrac{7x^2 + 3}{5}}$$
15	$$3\left(x - \dfrac{7}{6}\right)^2 + \dfrac{131}{12}$$
16	$$2n^3$$
17	$$x = \dfrac{21}{2} \pm \sqrt{\dfrac{469}{2}}$$
18	$$x = 4 \pm \sqrt{\dfrac{40}{3}}$$
19	$x = 1.2$ and $y = 9.2$ OR $x = 4$ and $y = 5$ Both needed
20	$$fhg(x) = 18x^2 + 147x + 314$$
21	$$n^3 - n^2 + 3$$

22	$x < -3, x > \frac{1}{2}$
23	$-7 \leq x \leq 3$
24	(graph: parabola crossing x-axis at -5 and 9)
25	(graph: parabola with minimum at $y = 7$)
26	

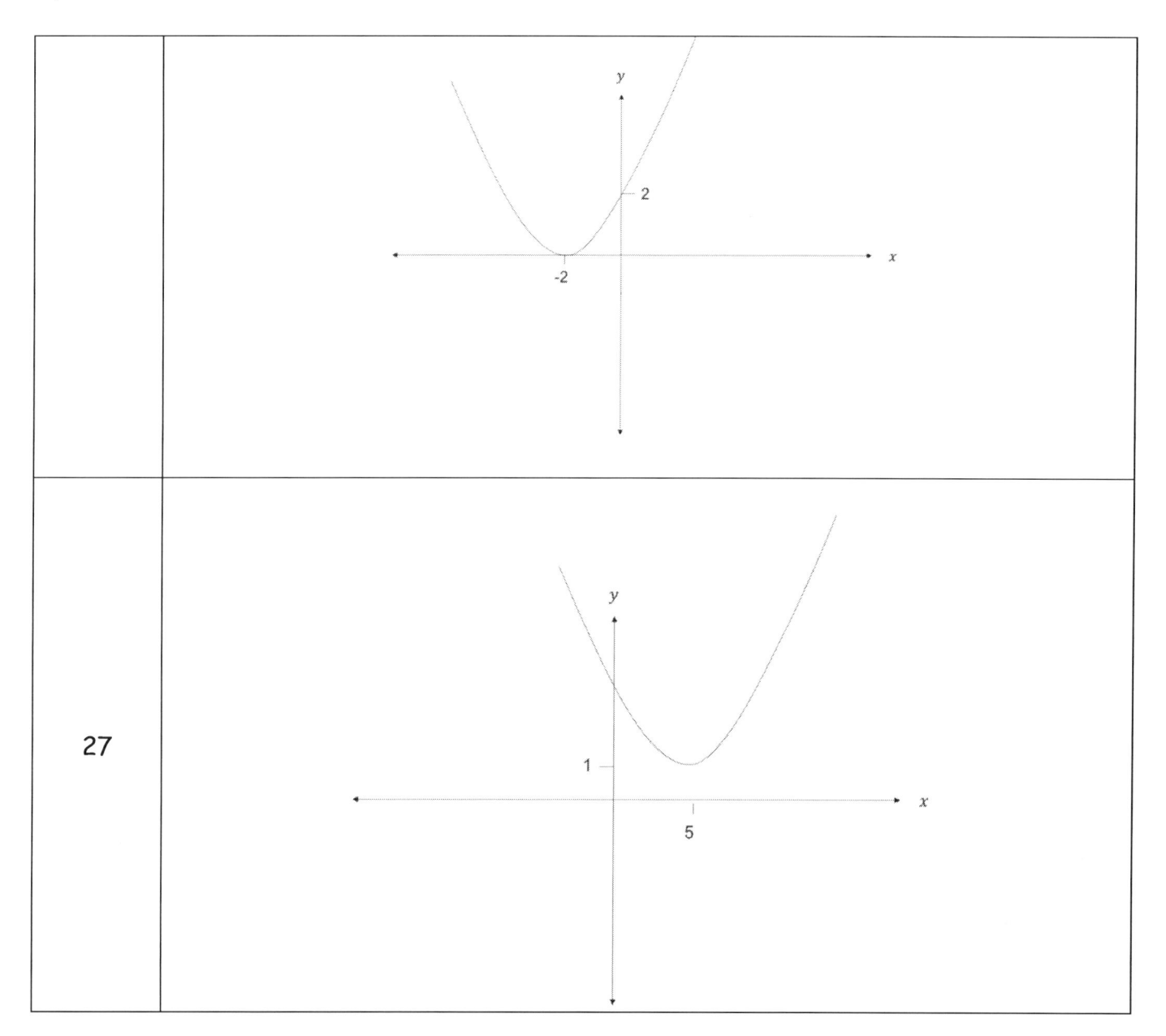

27

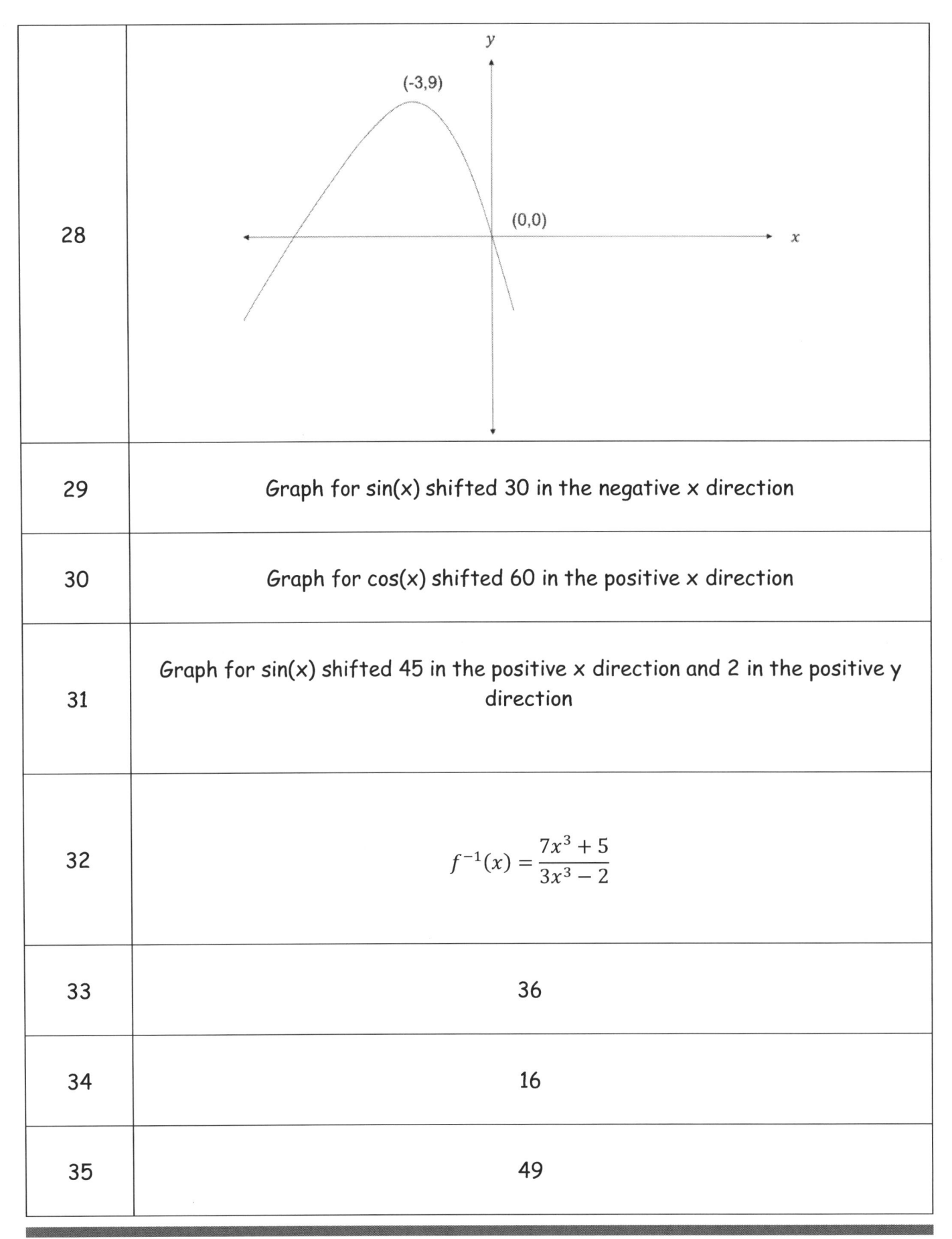

28	(graph of downward parabola with maximum at (-3,9) passing through (0,0))
29	Graph for sin(x) shifted 30 in the negative x direction
30	Graph for cos(x) shifted 60 in the positive x direction
31	Graph for sin(x) shifted 45 in the positive x direction and 2 in the positive y direction
32	$f^{-1}(x) = \dfrac{7x^3 + 5}{3x^3 - 2}$
33	36
34	16
35	49

36	$y = -\frac{7}{4}x + \frac{65}{4}$
37	$16(n^4 + 2n^3 + n^2)$
38	$3(n^3 + 3n^2 + 5n + 3)$
39	$h = \frac{12\sqrt{5} + 6}{19}$
40	$\frac{x^2 + 8x + 7}{2x - 10}$
41	$(3x - 5)(2x + 7)$
42	$e = \frac{7(t - 2a^2)^3}{5}$
43	$x = 0, \quad x = -\frac{1}{3}, \quad x = \frac{7}{4}$
44	$y = \frac{8}{3}x + \frac{52}{3}$
45	a=3, b=2, c=4
46	x=-0.21 or x=-2.46 (both needed)
47	

Primrose Kitten – YouTube Tutorials for Science and Maths.

	x=12.08 or x=-0.08 (both needed)
48	V=7.7
49	$2(6n^2 + 18n) + 35$
50	$f^{-1}(4) = \dfrac{11}{3}$
	Good luck in your exam!! ☺

Printed in Great Britain
by Amazon